Credit Sales
&
Accounts Receivable
Management
(The Heart of an Organization's Very Survival!)

Gerard Assey

Credit Sales
&
Accounts Receivable
Management

By
Gerard Assey

© Copyright 2023 by Author

Published by:
Gerard Assey
19/18, Palli Arasan Street
Anna Nagar East
Chennai - 600 102

ISBN: 978-93-92492-45-7

Table of Contents

Introduction

The last few years, saw many businesses enjoy a booming economy, and during these good times, it's all too easy for businesses to get lax about receivables- with cash management often getting overlooked, taking a backstage, until it begins to pinch hard and feel where it hurts. Managing credit sales and accounts receivables therefore must be a top priority for every business.

You could have probably laid your hands on this book at such a time, or at a time when all over the world is full of negative statistics, warnings, and dire economic projections or you know of a recession coming up soon, or you just simply want to learn the strategies that can otherwise help you weather through any storm or tough time that your organization is going though...then this is the right book for you!

Remember: "Effective Credit Management (which includes Accounts Receivables) is the heart of an organizations very survival"

Many studies carried out on the growing sickness in industries and businesses reveal that BAD DEBT is the ONE major cause for bankruptcy. In a successful and vibrant economy, selling on credit has a number of advantages, especially when it generates a larger volume of business as well as widens one's market share. In fact, selling on credit often 'Makes' or 'Breaks' a sale and at most times gives one that edge over competition. Yet, one cannot afford to take this area of credit sales and accounts receivables management so lightly, as too many companies everyday are mounting with debts that are increasingly doubtful of recovery. The most precarious risk therefore to a company's profit on the sale is by way of interest expense from delayed collection. In essence, that is what credit management is all about and its objective can be said *"to have the highest possible debtors (sales) for the shortest possible time (collection/profit)".*

Has it ever occurred to you that before the customer buys one's goods both are interested - he in need of your goods and you in collecting the value of goods sold ie; the money; but once he gets the goods on credit, he is 'no more' interested in fulfilling his obligation of paying. It's only you (for your money!).

A company can have the finest product, a superb sales record and the most dedicated workforce, but if it does not get paid for its goods sold (.... and on time!) it will die. An unpaid debt is an unsecured loan being financed by your company (we can't even call it a loan, because on a loan one earns interest. We'll probably have to change the activity to 'charities'!). It means that many companies are prevented from achieving their full potential, because instead of using borrowed money to develop and grow their businesses, they now have to borrow money just to fund their own sales ledgers (in other words their customers). When you no longer control your debtors, the cost of financing your company's cash flow is at the mercy of those very same debtors.

If a business wishes to survive and prosper in today's economic environment it must pay close attention to all the factors which affect and takes care of its cash flow.

Credit Sales, Accounts Receivables and Cash flow Management in its broadest sense, relates to the planning, monitoring and controlling of factors affecting the rate and amount of cash that flows in and out of a business. The amount of cash available to a business depends on its trading performance, balance-sheet control, capital expenditure, dividend policy and the amount of borrowing and capital available. The rate of cash flow depends on the efficiency with which the business manages its stocks, debtors and creditors.

Managing Credit and Collecting Money (your Accounts Receivables), on time, every time, therefore are the 2 most important and vital factors which decide the fate of any business!

Key Reasons to make Credit Sales and Accounts Receivables as a TOP Priority for your Business:

As you focus on the future of your business, here are some powerful reasons to focus on the health of your receivables, especially during these down times

- ✓ Predictions confirm that outstanding receivables will rise further, thus making credit sales and accounts Receivables as a top function for CFO's to enhance liquidity and optimize working capital.
- ✓ Managing invoices especially the unpaid ones and past due receivables cost a lot- making businesses to suffer in a number of ways and can even pull down the entire business.
- ✓ A consistent and steady cash flow will keep businesses all oiled up and running smoothly enabling one to plan a future of growth including hiring more employees, investing in other companies, expanding product lines, and more.
- ✓ And if looking for VC's, a solid cash flow and good financial records will make one look good to investors.

✓ By working on past-due amounts quickly and professionally it will help maintain positive relationships with clients especially during these times when everyone is looking to grab a piece of someone else's pie

This book: **'Credit Sales & Accounts Receivable Management'** would therefore, essentially help you do just that by covering the necessities of credit sales, accounts receivables and cash flow management right from an understanding of how bad debt occurs with methods to prevent the same, through the steps of an effective collection call (both on phone and face to face) with emphasis on the importance of documentation, reports, procedures for systematic follow-up; including series of email letters and general tips for chasing your money too, especially in these precarious times, by encouraging proactive methods!

What are the KEY Objectives of this Book?

✓ To ensure that the reader is equipped with the necessary skills in collecting/zeroing on the accounts receivables, while YET keeping the customer and building up on the relationship using a professional approach.

✓ To ensure that you are equipped with the necessary tools to manage /control/ monitor collections on a day- to- day basis.

✓ To provide first, a thorough understanding of a recession, the signs and impact it has on businesses, how bad debt occurs, and how to prevent it.

✓ To ensure that the reader has an understanding of their own behavior pattern, thus enabling them understand others, especially customers, resulting in a good rapport, leading to collection of payments while building lasting relationships

Basically to sum up… the **4 How's**!

- ✓ ***HOW*** *bad debt occurs (everyone needs to understand the impact of this on the organization)*
- ✓ ***HOW*** *to prevent (prevention is better than cure!)*
- ✓ ***HOW*** *to collect your money…and finally*
- ✓ ***HOW*** *to keep your customer!*

From all of these objectives, you will notice that the primary objective of your collection effort is to bring the account current and, at the same time, to keep the account as a customer. Harassment by mail, in person or on telephone is generally not advisable and successful in collecting money or in retaining the account. But, by applying the proven techniques and preventive measures covered in this book, you can look forward to greater success in reducing your outstanding receivables, while yet retaining your customer, together with the added benefit of staying professional while also enjoying a pleasant, personal and rewarding experience.

By the time you finish reading the book, you would have learnt to manage credit, using planned preventive measures (the most vital part!), would have learnt to develop a complete systematic collection program, gained confidence in collecting your receivables and have acquired several new ideas for immediate use, including taking back an Action Plan which can be put to immediate practice.

This book is intended to help everyone whose job includes responsibility for managing sales, credit, and collecting money from customers. It is designed for any type of business- the small or big businesses, the credit sales, control and accounts receivables personnel, as well as for those who would just like to increase their knowledge of the subject.

However, the book is primarily targeted to meet the urgent need of every businessman or manager, as almost every organization today is faced with this major problem of 'Bad or Doubtful Debt' and how to cope with it, especially during these downtimes- to help survive and thrive into the future, enabling businesses successfully navigate the uncertainty and outperform the competition- **emerging profitable and victorious!**

Part 1-How Bad Debt Occurs:
The Cash Flow Cycle

The figure below clearly illustrates the cash flow cycle in any business. As can be seen the success of any business depends on how fast the money is collected and how smooth is the cash flow…

The CASHFLOW Cycle

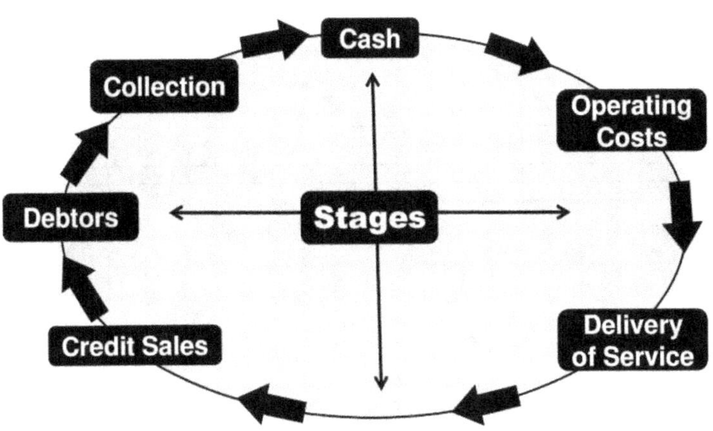

If a business wishes to survive and prosper in today's economic environment it must pay close attention to all the factors which affect its cash flow. Cash flow is the movement of money within a business, both Income and Expenditure, and is the key for business survival and growth.

Cash flow in the broadest sense, relates to the planning, monitoring and controlling of factors affecting the rate and amount of cash that flows in and out of your business. The amount of cash available to a business depends on its trading performance, balance-sheet control, capital expenditure, dividend policy and the amount of borrowing and capital available. The rate of cash flow depends on the efficiency with which the business manages its stocks, debtors and creditors. Cash, together with stocks, debtors and creditors makes up a business' working capital.

Here is a simple example:

Sales= 5000
Cost= 4500
Profit= 500

Month	January	February	March	April	May	June	July
Sales	5,000	5,000	5,000	5,000	5,000	5,000	5,000
Collection	0	0	0	0	0	0	0
Outstanding	5,000	10,000	15,000	20,000	25,000	30,000	35,000

As can be seen from above, in just one month...

Goods sold for a total value of	5000
Interest charged end of 1st month (18% or 1.5% per month)	75
Total costs one month	**5075**

Month two	5075
Interest charges month two (18% or 1.5% per month on 5075)	76
Total end of month two	**5151**

Month three	5151
Interest charges month three (18% or 1.5% per month on 5151)	77
Total end of month three	**5228**

(For the purpose of this exercise, we move on and see what happens if the account was to remain outstanding for seven months)

Month seven	5467
Interest charges month seven (18% or 1.5% per month on 5467)	82
Total end of month seven	**5549**

Gross profit from original purchase of 5000	500
Total lost on interest charges	549
Net loss	**49**

This is only an example for just one months working. So you could imagine how the entire profit is eroded now in a span of 7 months

Cash flow problems are the root cause for over 70% of businesses to fail within their first year...and it is the main reason for business failure.

Before we get any further, it is important for us to understand the very obvious question of: **'Why do businesses need cash'** in the first place?

- ✓ To meet all commitments/expenditures on time.
- ✓ To secure good rates / discounts
- ✓ To beat down suppliers with cash
- ✓ For expansion / diversification
- ✓ To purchase new assets
- ✓ Develop newer products/ invest in R & D
- ✓ To pay its taxes & other statutory requirements

Can you think of any other reasons now?

The Slide to Insolvency

How and why do businesses slide into a state of insolvency?

A very common scenario today is to see 'Yesterday's Cash Rich Companies' sliding into a state of insolvency today! In every business what one really earns is the net margin and could vary from industry to industry. Assuming it is around 25%, and if one fails to recover the payment from the due invoice, then not only has the business lost this net margin, but also their own investment into the cost of producing the said goods, resulting in the chances of this business going into danger.

Most organizations that fail to pay their creditors usually show one or a number of early warning signs, but one should be cautious and not act on just any one piece of information. Watch out for them early enough!

Here is a list of some of those 'insolvency warning/ danger signs' that can alert you well ahead of time.

- ✓ Deteriorating record in payment pattern (later and later each month)
- ✓ A new signatory-especially if new signatory not known
- ✓ Signatories away for longer than two weeks
- ✓ Customer's product constantly changing
- ✓ Customer's premises in disarray-stock levels low/ or too high (no movement)
- ✓ Rumors in the industry, from customers staff, your sales staff, market, other creditors

- ✓ Customer will not accept reasonable resolvement of queries
- ✓ Offers to pay part now and part later
- ✓ Cheque just never comes (Says…It's in the post/ courier!)
- ✓ Promises persistently broken
- ✓ People avoiding you -always in meetings
- ✓ People never ring back- poor response
- ✓ When time to pay, raises excuses that certificates like inspection/ test-not attached (raises lame excuses)
- ✓ Always referred to someone else
- ✓ Feedback on large borrowings
- ✓ Round sum cheques
- ✓ Essential bills not paid-electricity, rents, telephone, salaries etc
- ✓ Dispute with partners/ board level
- ✓ Shifting to SAP/ ERP/ RTGS
- ✓ Post dated cheques
- ✓ More than one mistake on cheques
- ✓ Contra claims are made
- ✓ Goods received in damaged condition / short received
- ✓ Unnaturally large orders – Over stocking than the requirement
- ✓ High staff turnover/ Discontent in staff/ downsizing
- ✓ Vendors waiting at the reception
- ✓ Plan or rumor of transfer of ownership
- ✓ Office moved from a posh location
- ✓ Press comments-resignations of key personnel, disputes, product failures, tax authority raids etc
- ✓ Complains about service
- ✓ Something in the 'voice'

- ✓ Frequent change of banks
- ✓ Change of premises/ address
- ✓ Change of telephone numbers

Bad Debt- A Major Profit Leak!

How much does bad debt cost?
Did you know that a 5000 bad debt can actually cost your company 50,000 or even 200,000? Well it's true!

If your profit margin is 10%, you will have to find 50,000 worth of new business to make good for that 5000 bad debt. If your profit margin is only 2.5% you will need to generate 200,000 worth of new business just to be in the position you were in before you suffered from a 5,000 bad debt. That's without considering what you spent in terms of time and effort chasing the debt and what about the other more obvious costs like collectors, solicitors or for the time the salesman had to go round to try and get a cheque, all the phone calls and letters your staff had to do etc. All in all you could have spent another 5000 only to watch as the debtor went into liquidation and you get nothing as a result. If you had only been tighter on credit control or recognized the warning signs sooner!.

Regular credit reviews are essential and don't fall into the old trap of being tough on new customers but relaxing after a couple of years for older "more reliable ones" because they had been good payers. Treat every customer as though they are on probation and you may just save yourself that 200,000, or even stop your own company from sinking because it is a fact that bad debts force more companies to fail than any other reason.

How money is lost every day!
By now we are convinced that bad debt is a major profit leak. So let us examine and study how our money is lost every day.
From studying the processes in various organizations, following are some of the main areas of leaks:
- ✓ Insufficient or no follow up.
- ✓ Improper / inaccurate / no documentation.
- ✓ Delay in submission of invoice.
- ✓ Interest on over dues/Interest on borrowings.
- ✓ Cost of administration (Collection cost for recovery of money)
- ✓ Our focus on defaulters (waste of time!)-not on new customers!
- ✓ Cheque floats (delay in cheque clearances)-A bank problem!
- ✓ Time lag for depositing of cheques (lethargy in office / internal office procedures)
- ✓ Cheque bounces
- ✓ Unclear trade terms/ not documented or spelt out
- ✓ Statutory amounts already paid up by you-not yet recovered! (eg; taxes etc)
- ✓ Improper training for collection personnel.
- ✓ Depreciating currency/ Time value of money (Due to inflation… Money banked after a period of credit does not have the same purchasing power as money banked at delivery of goods)
- ✓ The loss due to exchange (fluctuation) of currency (in case of foreign currency)
- ✓ Bill Discounting with bankers, on open credit, but payment not met by customers on due date

✓ Risk of losing or writing off

An Example of Declining Value of Overdue Accounts

Current debtors are worth	100%
30 days overdue debts are worth	98%
90 days overdue debts are worth	94%
180 days overdue debts are worth	88%
One Years overdue debts are worth	76%
Three Years overdue debts are worth	28%

Hence sundry debtors over 3 years are worth NIL (Discounted at Bank Interest of 24% pa, taken as a hypothetical example only, plus other factors)

Remember that your cash flow is the fuel in the engine that drives your business! And delinquent accounts are the brakes that bring companies to a screeching halt, leading to even file bankruptcy.

The probability of full collection on a delinquent account drops dramatically with the length of delinquency.

These are the chances you can take on each account:

On the due date:	94.9 % chance
30 days past due:	89.9 % chance
60 days past due:	81.3 % chance
90 days past due:	69.6 % chance
Six months:	52.1 % chance
Nine months:	39.1 % chance
One year:	22.8 % chance
Two years:	9.3 % chance

For example, even after only three months, the probability of collecting a delinquent account drops to 69.6 %. After six months, collectability drops to 52.1 % and after one year, the probability of ever collecting a delinquent account drops to 22.8 %. The results of this survey clearly demonstrate the crucial importance of taking immediate action when an account receivable ages past its due date.

Below you will find a study by the US Department of Commerce statistics that clearly illustrates how the age of each account determines its value, and the older it gets, the less likely you are to collect it!

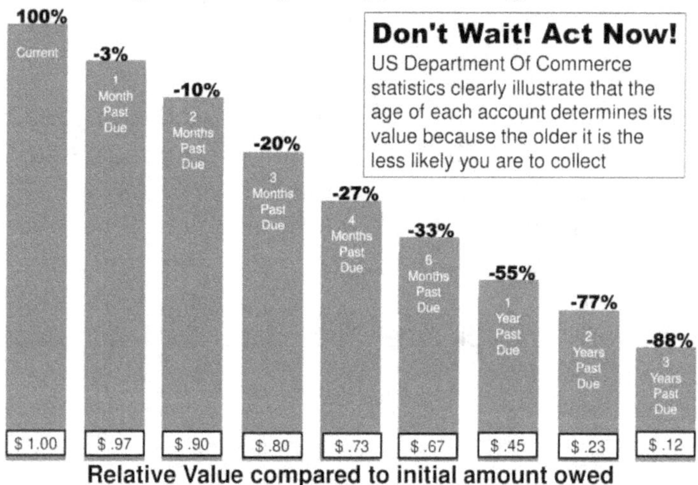

In another research, it was indicated that firms wait on an average of **78 days** for their bills to be paid, though payment terms were usually 30 days. The cost of financing this extra **48 days** is expensive-equivalent to **5.7% of turnover- more than 50% of net profit** in a number of businesses!

Don't think of years/months or weeks delay...because interest you pay for everyday-even

Sundays!!! In other words older the debt, greater is the chance of total loss.

A Company can have a superb sales record and most dedicated workforce, but if it does not get paid (on time!) it will lead to winding up. You build the company and customer winds it up.

Remember: An unpaid debt is an unsecured loan being financed by your company.

It means, many companies are prevented from achieving their full potential, because instead of using borrowed money to develop and grow their own business, they now have to borrow money just to fund their own sales ledgers.

Cash is therefore to business what blood is to the body. Allow it to drain away and the body becomes weak and eventually dies!

So what then do you think is the **ONE** major cause for Bad Debt?

In all my years of managing and leading some of the largest sales forces in the country, I have found the answer to be: **NO FOLLOW-UP at all stages!**

In reality, the sales team is after all more interested in procuring the next sales order than collecting the existing outstanding. The customer knows this weakness and keeps tempting with fresh orders (which costs him only an A4 paper) by delaying to pay your old dues.

So now the question is…What then makes the difference between a profitable business and one forced into liquidation, because of slow and default debts?

The answer is: **Good Cash Collection Procedures!**

As you will by now, get to understand that 'Good Cash Collection Procedures' are very much an internal requirement, while the 'Follow-up' part is an external one- and both of these must go hand in hand if your collection efforts are to be successful.

Debt Collecting is therefore:
At the heart of <u>your</u> organization's survival
At the heart of <u>your</u> relationship with your customer
And…A skill which <u>anyone</u> can learn and should possess!

What % of customers pay their bills promptly, before being asked?
Studies reveal that 10 % of people pay their bills promptly and without complaint, and those who don't pay promptly, broadly fall into 3 categories, showing why debt collecting is a skill with each situation requiring different handling techniques and skills:
- ✓ They always pay at the last possible moment
- ✓ They want to, but they can't at the moment
- ✓ They never intended to pay in the first place (there is always a very tiny % that fall in this category- they slip in if our credit control is not proper)

Why customers don't pay
- ✓ Deep Financial Liquidity Problem (Financial Crisis)
- ✓ Dissatisfaction (with service/ product/ treatment received by them, complaint or dispute pending etc)
- ✓ Purposeful Delay (Takes advantage-Trying to run their business with our unsecured interest-free debt)

- ✓ Inefficiency in <u>Their</u> Office Procedure (lost invoice, forgetful, no system for regular payments, unorganized etc)
- ✓ Inefficiency in <u>Our</u> Office Procedure (improper follow-up, lack of records/documentation etc)

Part 2-How to Prevent Bad Debt
Effective Credit Control- Preventive Measures

Before deciding to offer your goods or services on credit, there are few steps you would like to consider as 'Preventive Steps'
- ✓ Assessing the benefits (of providing credit) to your organization
- ✓ True cost of giving Credit: How much is it going to cost us? What is the repercussion? What are the risks? Where could we lose? Have we loaded the financial cost into the selling price?
- ✓ Set up a simple Credit Management System (Step by step from Credit Application, Terms, Credit limits, System to monitor collections, right up to chasing for collection of full payment –email letters, calls, visits- When, How many, tone/ message?)
- ✓ Invoices: Layout, Terms, Clauses covered!
- ✓ Categorize Customers/ Pareto's Principle
- ✓ Assess the Credit Worthiness of the Customer

Advantages of doing business on credit- To you as the Supplier
- ✓ Increases sales
- ✓ Increases liquidity/cash flow
- ✓ Increases profits
- ✓ Enhances purchasing power
- ✓ Enables increase in productivity
- ✓ Helps expand and promotes growth
- ✓ Better penetration- wider markets reached

✓ Overall- promotes growth

Assessing the 'True Cost' of Giving Credit
✓ Interest paid or Not received
✓ Depreciating currency
✓ Cost of Administration/ Collection costs
✓ Affects cash flow cycle/ Financing the receivables
✓ Increased risk of bad debt
✓ Business failure
✓ Statutory amounts already paid in advance by you
✓ Commitments made to others- affects your image!
✓ Affects balance sheet-Credibility with bankers/ Image
✓ Can lead to tension/headaches/sleepless nights!
✓ May limit one's expansion possibility- If funds are held up!

Various Stages in Credit Management
✓ Get 'Credit Application Form' (Whom are we selling to? You must have complete details- But make it quick & hassle-free)
✓ Evaluate creditworthiness of customer
✓ Decide credit rating and risk category. Tell everyone in your organization
✓ Set credit limits
✓ Define terms of payment
✓ Allocate an account number (no services until)
✓ Determine invoicing procedures
✓ Set up a system for recording and reporting amounts due

- ✓ Set-up methods for collecting amounts when due
- ✓ Send "Welcome Letter" to payments contact
- ✓ Keep track for 3 months (phone personally so that good payment habits develop & to avoid bad habits)

Here are few ways to 'Assess the Creditworthiness' of Customers (A Checklist)

- ✓ Past Records: Account experience: payment performance, sales, disputes, and trends.
- ✓ Sales Force Reports (In house opinion) sales visits regularly; aware of industry developments to pass on to you
- ✓ Bank Reference (Their banks may not divulge directly to you- but your banker could help you get from their banker)
- ✓ Trade Associations.
- ✓ Chambers of Commerce.
- ✓ Credit Rating Agencies/ CRISIL
- ✓ Market feedback.
- ✓ Visit to customers premise.
- ✓ Probe from secretaries/ reception/ watchmen/ drivers etc
- ✓ Press Reports: interim company results, resignations, topical data, labor strife
- ✓ Stock Exchange opinion
- ✓ Registrar of Companies (Annual Reports)
- ✓ Balance sheet analysis
- ✓ Customers' suppliers. (..check to see if they are paid on time)
- ✓ Life of Business (Industry growth rate, Technological changes? Performance trends?

- ✓ Nature of Business- Seasonal? Cyclic? Key success factors? Competition?
- ✓ Bank Balances (consistency)
- ✓ Customers negotiation power
- ✓ Credit card statements
- ✓ Rented/ Own premises
- ✓ PAN/TAN
- ✓ Security Deposit
- ✓ Reference checks/Introductions
- ✓ Trade Licenses/Sponsor (in some countries)
- ✓ Family Background
- ✓ Website/P.O. Box no. etc
- ✓ Assets
- ✓ Age of person (if he does not have a heir and privately owned, then you are in a problem)
- ✓ Eagerness to genuinely do a long term business

Your Invoice!

(The only purpose of an invoice is to claim payment.)

- ✓ Insist on your company having a simple, effective invoice document.
- ✓ Show clearly the date, reference and total.
- ✓ Have a good layout for description of services.
- ✓ Display your GST number/ Provision to add Customers' GST number
- ✓ Show the customer's order number
- ✓ Show the method of dispatch/ delivery.
- ✓ Attach proof of delivery
- ✓ Show the invoice due date in big/ bold letters.
- ✓ Show payment terms clearly- not hidden and not in tiny font

- ✓ Ensure customer's special instructions are followed
- ✓ Have a procedure for checking accuracy before signing
- ✓ Cut out all unnecessary data, which only serves to obscure the important data.
- ✓ Most of all show clearly the payment terms and penalty for late-payment.

A few suggestions you can ensure to tighten your credit policy

- ✓ Have every customer sign a credit application and check their credit-thoroughly before proceeding to do business with them!
- ✓ Be clear on the terms of your deal; always obtain it in writing!
- ✓ If you extend credit, monitor the accounts for overdue payments, and have a system to keep them up to date.
- ✓ Have a penalty for past-due balances, such as a late fee or termination of credit privileges. (The word around in the market should know that you are not slack!)
- ✓ The following are questions to ask yourself about your delinquent customers in order to limit your credit risk:

  Are they in a position to pay in full?

  Will they be in a position to pay your bill in 3 months?

  What will you do if they can't pay you?

  How will you pay your bills if your customers are delinquent?

  What other options can you think of?

Categorizing your Customers

Your system must have a means to categorize your customers.

Why categorize customers? So you will be able to keep track and accordingly handle them with the relevant skills, techniques and treatment, depending on the category that they belong to.

Here is a simple yet powerful method to categorize your customers:

Categorizing your Customers

Category	% to Total	No of Accounts	Who? (The List)
A			
B			
C			
D			
E			

A-Those that pay before time

B-Those that pay on time

C-Those that pay little beyond credit period (tolerance limit)

D-Those that pay after a lot of effort & energy (but will pay!)

E-Those that say: *'Do what you want- I will not pay!'*

Effective Credit Management is being able to move customers from E to A by doing all we can to retain A in that position!

Coding your Customers

Prior to categorizing your customers, you must allocate codes for each customer.

Why would coding customers be important? Before we actually get into seeing the benefits of this, let us look at a sample as given below:

Coding your Customers

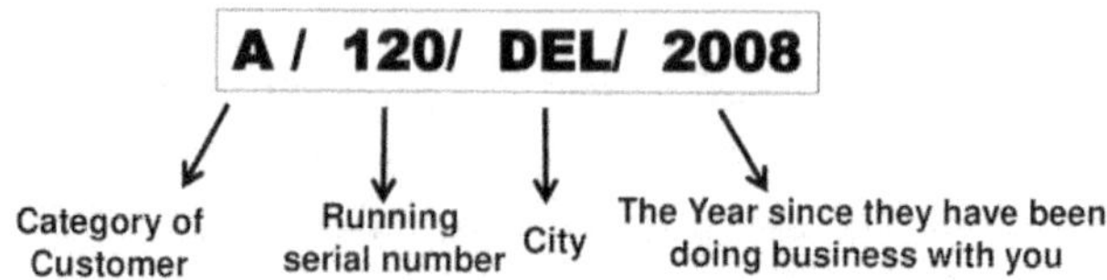

- ✓ The above sample has four fields, but I have clients that have taken this method and creatively gone up to eight fields on their system.
- ✓ As you will notice, the first field (the category) can change. An example would be: when a customer joined in, due to his prompt payment record, he was classified as A, but as time went by he slipped to category B. All other fields would remain constant without change.
- ✓ In the third field, if all the customers are in one city, then this could be changed to the pin code.
- ✓ You can take the above coding further by using flags on your customer accounts as provided below

Flags on Customer Accounts

- ✓ Flags are a very important part of credit management.
- ✓ There are two types of credit accounts. The first category is of all of the accounts that owe you money with no reason whatsoever not to pay.
- ✓ The other is where- those with queries, awaiting credit, complaints, damaged goods

etc. This group must be 'flagged' on your system to identify them from the first group.

- ✓ If you do not flag the second group you will not be able to identify where your problems are.
- ✓ If an account has a query put a 'Q' before or after the account number:
- ✓ The letter 'D' for 'damaged' goods, a 'C' for awaiting 'credit' ... and so forth. You may wish to add letters such as 'N' which indicates that the customer is 'New': Or 'C' for 'Complaint: 'H' for on 'Hold', etc. These letters are called 'flags'. They indicate special circumstances: no flag means all is in order and the account is clear.
- ✓ You can create your own coding, and by looking at the account anyone should be able to understand the current status of the account

Benefits of coding your customers

There are several good reasons why you should have a good code for each customer and here are some:

- ✓ Helps in sorting customers
- ✓ Just looking at the code, you will be able to know how long they have been with you
- ✓ It will help you manage your territory/ area-wise
- ✓ If you are looking at any special gifts/schemes, it would help you provide such preferential treatment for different categories
- ✓ For emailing of reminder letters – this can help you target the specific category
- ✓ This can also provide you with an indication of a customer's payment history at a glance-

showing you how and when they slipped from a good paying category into another category
- ✓ If a sales/ collection person is in front of a particular customer (say a defaulter) and needs to talk to his manager, then this code can help indicate to the manager, instead of the collector having to provide any further details

Part 3 & 4-How to Collect your Money & Keep your Customer
Having a Proper Strategy for Collection

All collection efforts must be planned with proper strategies. Failure to do so can be like trying to find a pin in the dark. Given below are a few ideas on creating a strategy that can help you develop your own in-house ones.

An Example of a proper strategy for collection
- ✓ Declare an 'Emergency' (In other words- let everyone know in the organization, the importance of collecting money- have periodic campaigns)
- ✓ Make everyone responsible- (Emphasize on the importance for everyone to co-operate)
- ✓ Set up a special 'Task Force' (With top management support- along with a special representative from each and every department- to ensure that this representative co-ordinates/liaises with his/ her respective department in ensuring a smooth working)
- ✓ Assess skills of personnel on the team
  - On phone / In person
  - Documentation
  - Provide necessary trainings where required- so all are equipped
- ✓ Identify problem- In value / number / age

- ✓ Break into controllable units with each individuals responsibility
- ✓ Set targets for each person – Should be achievable and just
- ✓ Plan action-Using different techniques – Visits'/Phone Calls/ Reminders
- ✓ Run blitz for a specific time period (say 8 Weeks?)
- ✓ Monitor results -Every week analyze variance and short falls
- ✓ Work out action plan to pick up shortfall
- ✓ Share % on collection
- ✓ Celebrate success!

Implementing the Collection Program

(Sample for a 30 days credit period)

Day 1:   Send Invoice both by email and hard copy by courier

Day 26: Send 'Polite' reminder stating payment due on 30th Day (Together with statement)

Day 29: Make a telephone call reminding that payment is due tomorrow

Continue chase everyday on phone.

Day 35: Send "Past due Reminder Email"

Day 45: Send "Second Mildly Aggressive- When an invoice is long overdue" Reminder Letter

Day 50: Continue Telephone Chasing Everyday (Or Other Action- Email or SMS to Sr. People)

Day 60: Final Action "'Final Notice' Email" Stop Services / Refer to Collection Agency

REMEMBER: *THE SOONER YOU ASK - THE SOONER YOU GET PAID!*

Understanding the 'Benefits of Paying on Time'
The key to getting your customers to paying you on time is for them to understand the importance of the key benefits to them by doing so.

What are the benefits to your customers for paying on time? Here are a few:
- ✓ Avoiding interest payment/ penalties
- ✓ Protecting credit rating
- ✓ Avoiding service / late charges
- ✓ Ensuring continuity in service/Uninterrupted service
- ✓ Better terms and rates for prompt payers
- ✓ Taking advantage of special offers
- ✓ Pride and Image
- ✓ Goodwill in Market
- ✓ Special R&D for the customer
- ✓ Preferential treatment
- ✓ Special packaging/labeling for customer
- ✓ No further credit rating required for his recommendations
- ✓ Extended warranties
- ✓ Free training on use of products
- ✓ Free POP/ Publicity material
- ✓ Help in selling or movement of stock
- ✓ Keeping the relationship going
- ✓ Avoidance of disturbance/Peace of life

Effectively using Email/ Letters for your Debt Collections

Today, very few organizations actually use snail mail, especially when it comes to debt collections- so forget about snail mail. It's just a waste of your time and more importantly, your customer's time, while delaying the collection process too. On the other hand, email if used correctly, is an incredibly powerful tool to improve the efficiency of your debt collection process- with about 80% of your unpaid invoices that can be successfully collected with just the right emails. Structured and timely emails will not only save you time, but can help reduce the amount of outstanding debt that you have.

As the invoice ages, you will need to adjust the tone of your email with customers. The email will need to make the customer understand that this is becoming a serious issue for your organization and that failure to solve the issue will have negative consequences. Your communication however, does not need to be hostile or harsh, but can still reinforce your commitment to working with them to resolve the issue.

Initial approach by letter- Why?

- ✓ Though a phone call is more effective -a letter has certain advantages:
- ✓ It's more polite to make initial contact by letter rather than straight away by phone
- ✓ Many customers will respond to a letter– and for a number of bills outstanding, it will help get the telephone 'hit list' down to a manageable size

- ✓ If there are problems later – the fact that you lodged a letter makes your position stronger
- ✓ Finally – if your letter isn't replied to, it gives a good excuse to phone!

How and what should your reminder letters have or do?

Areas to be considered for reminder letters:
- ✓ Purpose (ensure they have one objective- to get payment. Never mix content with any other subject. It dilutes the effect)
- ✓ The number (Ideally not more than four- beyond that would let the customer start to take you lightly, and ignore them)
- ✓ Content and design (On your letterhead, if by hard copy- courier or post)
- ✓ Frequency and timing
- ✓ 1st letter- Polite, yet assertive
- ✓ 2nd letter- Mildly aggressive
- ✓ 3rd letter- Positively threatening
- ✓ 4th letter- I'LL FIX YOU- NOW!

Letters should be:

- ✓ Individually typed (not photocopied- if being sent by courier/ post)
- ✓ Addressed to a named person (personalized)
- ✓ Signed – not "pp'd" (if a hard copy is being sent)
- ✓ Not more than a page in length
- ✓ Use simple, uncomplicated words
- ✓ Use a larger font to highlight the important parts of your letter-such as the balance that is due, the past days or the action you may take
- ✓ Sent by recorded delivery- if hard copy (creates a psychological effect)

- ✓ With all details- invoice no / sales order / date/ amount / when due etc
- ✓ Without reference to passage of time (e.g. Not 'within 10 days'- But say 'pay by 12th Nov')
- ✓ Keeping possibilities open – avoid empty threats!

Sample Email Letters

Here are a few sample emails along with when these should be sent for maximum effectiveness.

Let us start on a positive note. So let's begin with a 'Thank you' for the payment.

Key: Always thank the customer as soon as you've received the payment!

A 'thank you note' can go a long way. When an invoice is cleared, whether it was early, on time, or even later, you should always have a practice of sending the customer a *"thanks for the payment"* email. The result of this will always be positive; and does several things: the customer will either feel guilty about their late payment from your polite and courteous dealing of it and make efforts to pay earlier in future, or they will appreciate you recognizing them paying in a timely manner, reinforcing and bonding the relationship; ensuring future payments too on time.

For this 'thank you' email to be really effective and achieve its purpose, it must be addressed to specific personnel by name and copied to the relevant authorities involved in the whole process, as the objective is solely for relationship-building and encouraging positive behavior by appreciating clients while also being firm.

Example
Subject: (*Your business' name/ invoice (Invoice reference number/ Amount*)

Body:
Dear (Recipient's name)

This short note is just to let you know that we have received your recent payment in respect of invoice (invoice reference number) for the amount of (mention amount).
Thank you very much. We sincerely appreciate it.

With best wishes,
(Sender's name/ title)

1. Pre-Due Reminder Email

Before an invoice is due, there's only one goal that you would need to focus on doing – to ensure the conditions are suitable for your customer to be able to make payment on or before time. You should remind customers a few days before the invoice is due to pay you. Ideally, this can be 3-5 days before the invoice due date. You can use this to politely enquire if everything is okay for the customer to make payment by the due date. This method prevents the customer from coming up with any excuses on the payment due date, while also ensuring that your invoice is fresh in their mind and difficult to "forget" to pay; it also goes a long way in helping to build and maintain a great working relationship.

Example:
Subject: Your business Name/ Invoice details (*Invoice reference number with Amount/ due date*)

Body:
Dear *(Recipient's name) (Avoid a Hi or Hello!)*

I hope you are doing well.
I just wanted to send you this quick note to remind you that (amount owed on invoice) in respect of our invoice (invoice reference number) is due for payment on (date due).
I would be really grateful if you could confirm that everything is on track for payment to be released by the said date.

You can CLICK HERE to go to our website to pay or use the several options mentioned below to make payment.
(List all options here)

Kindly disregard this email if payment has already been processed.

Best regards
(Sender's full name/ Title)

A **clear, crisp and concise subject line** gets their immediate attention. With most inboxes limiting the subject line to just a few words, it is important to say as much as you can with as little text as possible. Think for a moment of the volume of emails your recipient receives per day- you are literally fighting a battle to get your email on top, noticed and worked on by them.

Studies have proven that the combination of your business name and the invoice reference number is required to get their attention. It lets the recipient know precisely who is communicating (in this case, your business' name) and what this email refers to.

When you word this first email as being casual (*"just wanted to send you this quick note"*) it helps go a long way to diffuse any potential of being interpreted as harassing them about payment at this stage itself. And remember-before you hit the send button; always attach a copy of the invoice and current statement of accounts. If they already have your invoice or statement of account on hand, no harm done, and it doesn't cost you anything, but this method prevents payments from getting held up by customers turning back to say *"oh, we actually did not receive that invoice as yet…"* or *" We need an updated statement of accounts"*

2. Past due Reminder Email

As the due date for payment passes, you will need to adjust the tone of your email now with such customers. Invoices that have past beyond your payment terms need to be followed up immediately, ideally within 2-3 business days. This 'Past due Reminder' email should be sent conveying to the customer of the past due balance with a slightly more serious tone. While your tone needs to become more assertive since the first letter seems to have gone ignored, you still need to remain friendly towards the customer. Finding the right balance between being assertive and friendly is always difficult. The customer needs to understand that this is becoming a serious issue and that failure to pay may result in consequences. And not only helping your image out in the marketplace (that you are serious about business and not a charitable organization) in the long run, your customer will actually respect you for it and if they don't, they're probably not the right customer and not worth doing business with in the future.

The objective here is to positively but firmly communicate that there are outstanding payments due, through this past due payment reminder email.

Example:
Subject: Your business Name/ Invoice
details (*Invoice reference number with amount - Past X Days!*)

Body:
Dear (Recipient's name) (Avoid a Hi or Hello!)

We have yet to receive our payment from your organization of (amount owed on invoice) in respect of our invoice (invoice reference number) which was due for payment on (date due).
We understand that oversights happen but would appreciate immediate payment of this amount, which is now already overdue. May we remind you of our payment terms agreed by you and listed on our invoice? As a valued customer, we would like to help you quickly remit payment to avoid your credit rating or future credit limits with our company be affected. If there is any reason you are unable to pay in full, please contact me on 12345678

In the meanwhile, you can CLICK HERE to go to our website to pay or use the several options mentioned below.
(list all options here)

We thank you in advance for paying promptly.

Best regards,
(Sender's full name/ Title)

Note that this second email is very specific that you want *"immediate"* payment. You are quite specifically telling them that you want the payment immediately and you are reminding them of your terms and the consequences as a result of non-payment or further delays. As with your previous email, remember to attach a copy of the invoice again along with current statement of accounts.

3. When an invoice is long overdue

If you've chased a customer repeatedly for an overdue unpaid invoice without any result, it's now time to change your collection tactics. The key here is to let the customer know that late payment is not okay with you, by adding a strong element of urgency to the payment reminder. Therefore the objective is a strong mail for overdue payment while yet in a professional manner.

Example:

Subject: Your business Name/ Invoice
details (*Invoice reference number with amount –
LONG OVERDUE!)*

Body:

Dear (Recipient's name) (No Hi or Hello!)

We have as of date yet to receive payment from your organization, despite our earlier reminders (on dates), for (amount owed on invoice) in respect of our invoice (invoice reference number) which was long overdue for payment on (date due)
This invoice is now (number of days overdue) days overdue and is becoming really a matter of serious concern for us. As already having reminded you of our payment terms that were agreed upon by you and listed on our invoice, we are now concerned that our credit terms have been significantly exceeded and therefore we are unable to provide any further service to you until payment is made, while hoping that we will not be put in the position of having to take stronger action.
I hope to hear from you before this action is taken, to avoid affecting your credit rating or our future business relationship. Please contact me immediately at 12345678 so we can get this matter settled.

With best regards
(Sender's first name/ Title)

As with the other samples so far, you will note that this still covers the key principles of politeness, while yet letting the customer know that late payment is not okay-and is achieved with the line describing the late payment as *"becoming really a matter of serious concern for us."* This hits into the customer's guilt about paying late but without getting aggressive or attacking them. Doing the latter will only put them on the defensive and not help you achieve a mutually agreeable outcome at all, not to mention ending up in an unhealthy relationship.

The element of urgency is literally spelled out in the body as well, as made quite clear in the subject line with the words *"LONG OVERDUE"*.

Again, remember to attach a copy of the invoice, along with a statement of account to prevent getting any excuses even at this stage

4. 'Final Notice' Email

After all the above efforts with still no payment, then schedule this "Final Notice" email <u>only as a last and final</u> resort.

Example:

Subject: Your business Name/ Invoice details (*Invoice reference number with Amount- LONG PAST DUE*)

Body:
Dear (Recipient's name) (No Hi or Hello!)

Despite several reminders (on dates), we regret to inform you that we have as yet not received our due payment from your organization for (invoice amount owed) in respect of our invoice (invoice reference number) which was due for payment on (date due). This invoice is now (number of days overdue) days long past overdue and as you are aware, late payment penalties will now be added if payment is not received immediately. This matter may also be passed on to our legal department which may result in your loss of credit rating and/or further proceedings from their end.

You can CLICK HERE to go to our website to pay or use the several options mentioned below.
(list all options here)

Thanks in advance for your understanding and cooperation.

Best regards
(Insert Sender's Full Name/ Title)

In this email you clearly state what the repercussions are for non-payment. Again, remember to attach a copy of the invoice, along with statement of accounts.

A Key Point to Note for these types of customers would be to take recourse to the IBC (Insolvency & Bankruptcy Code) which in recent years, has given another powerful tool in the hands of the Collector of Debts to bring such incorrigible and recalcitrant customers to book.

Your Professional Image: Sell yourself before you sell anything else!

A very important part that we would be touching on now is that of how we communicate or the impressions we create even before we could open our mouths.

In a study carried out that I am about to share with you now, you will notice that people place more emphasis on what they SEE rather than on what they HEAR.

So this only tells us that we need to be very careful with our body language and what we are projecting.

According to studies carried out, Communication takes place in 3 forms:

Your Words

Your Tone and

Your Body Language.

Where 55% has to do with your BODY LANGUAGE or what others SEE.

7 % has to do with WHAT you say or your words

Whilst 38% has to do with HOW those words are said, which is your Tone or voice modulation

With people going by what they SEE first rather than what they HEAR, it makes it very important for us to therefore project the RIGHT image upfront. That's the impression that has been formed-good or bad! If it is good, then very good for you, but if it is bad, then so sad! Because…now you have double work to undo the wrong impression that has already gone into the mind and to now fill it with the right impression.

They say 90% of lasting impressions are created in the first 90 seconds. That can be really dangerous, but surprisingly that is true! So we have to be very careful, with what are we projecting as soon as someone sees us, because that's what they will remember. (Now you could be wondering why are we covering on body language, when the customer will not be seeing us if on phone…but hold on till the end of this chapter to know how this impacts your call!)

It is also a reason why we tend to remember a song seen on a television set better than when heard through a radio. The same logic applies at a job interview with your resume and the presentation of it! Then at the interview-the interviewer has made up his mind to a great extent as you walk in, even before you have opened your mouth. Your bio-profile or the interview process is only a confirmation of the decision already made in the mind of the interviewer.

Why is Tone next important after Body Language? Simply because you can say a same sentence with a different tone and that can change the entire meaning

Eg; *"Sarah come here"* is a simple sentence. But depending on the right tone this one sentence could turn out as an 'order 'or a 'request'.

Another stronger example: *"Hang him not let him go"*…could be death or life depending on how it is said. Example: *'Hang him, not let him go'!* Or *'Hang him not, let him go'!*

Now, if it is face to face, we may be able to save the situation, but when on the phone with the other person not able to see you, it could lead to miscommunication if the right tone is not used as seen from the examples just covered.

So here are a few aspects of voice quality that you can work on to improve your vocal image!

- ✓ Pitch/Tone: Too high, too low, ruff or irritating to the ear becomes noticeable and distracting. Record your voice, listen, work on improving vocal skills, and assess progress.
- ✓ Accent: Minimize your own accent and pick up the customer's speaking style, being clear and easily understood.
- ✓ Volume: Being too loud or too soft is a habit one can change. Ask how you sound.
- ✓ Inflection: One can impose their personal interpretation upon words by effective inflection. Use a natural inflection to maintain interest-Avoid monotone.
- ✓ Enthusiasm: Communicates a personal involvement in the conversation. Having a smile will enable this together with enabling you sound friendlier.
- ✓ Conveying emotions: Use your voice to convey confidence, enthusiasm, joy, friendliness, concern, or any other emotion.
- ✓ Sincerity: You must believe in what you are doing. Communicate your belief in yourself, company and product.
- ✓ Vocabulary: The right choice of words you use to communicate
- ✓ Pacing: It's the rate and rhythm of a speech pattern. Talk the same pace as that of your customer. Studies reveal that by simply 'mirroring' or 'echoing' a customer's pacing can increase the customers understanding of what is said.
- ✓ Pronunciation: Your ability to use the language correctly

As seen earlier, with people going by what they SEE first rather than what they HEAR, it makes it so very important for you to therefore project the RIGHT image upfront. It basically involves 'selling yourself first'!

Before a customer buys anything or decides to do business with you or the company that you represent, he needs to first be sold on you because you are what he sees about your company to him. Your company could have a several floor building, with several offices all across the globe. But to the customer what he sees in you, (through this call) is the impression he has formed of your company! Because…90% of lasting impressions are created in the first 90 seconds

Importance of maintaining a good posture when on the phone

If you slouch when you make a call, the prospect will actually be able to hear it in your voice. As well as impacting on the confidence and energy of the call, it can affect the tone of your voice. So before picking up the phone to call a prospect, collectors should ensure that their posture is right. Take a minute to ensure you are sitting up straight and have your shoulders back. This will instantly make you feel more energetic, more confident and more focused when you speak to the prospect.

Have all the data/ documentation for the call ready at hand. It is all about what the customer 'sees' about you as his first impression that enables him move forward. Use the gestures as if talking to someone physically in front of you. These gestures lead to facial expression and facial expressions affect the voice and the way the voice says the words. Try it!

Why the Right Attitude and Mindset is Most Important!

In any environment, whether at home or at work, the tendency to think positively and approach each and every task with a "can-do" attitude can be really infectious. Organizations are therefore very careful to have the right kind of people to prevent any potential problems among existing employees, as when it comes to selling or working in a team, the positive attitude can spill over into the way, enabling employees to cooperate with one another. On the other hand, employees with a poor attitude about the market, customers, work and the tasks they are required to complete will have a negative effect on those around them. Just as a positive attitude is infectious and spreads to others, so too will poor attitudes have a negative effect on employee relations, resulting in division in the workplace, making it difficult for employees to collaborate with one another, as the poor attitudes spill over into how they treat one another.

So what makes a Successful Collection Professional?

Being successful in debt collection is about being competent in a few key areas…So what are they?

While every business requires C.A.S.H. to survive and succeed….Every Debt Collection Professional also requires something in them in order to succeed, which I believe is more valuable than that CASH. This is 'K.A.S.H.' because only when you have this KASH in you, you will be more successful in bringing in the CASH for you and your company, while also resulting in retaining your customers for life'!

What is this KASH?
Knowledge
Attitude
Skills
Habits
Knowledge is all about your Company, the Products or Services that you offer, the Market and Industry that you operate in, together with knowing who are the other players or your competition that are in this industry. It also involves knowing where you stand against them-your strengths and areas that your competition has an advantage over you, along with being thorough on the rates, polices and regulations in your industry and market.
Some of the other areas under knowledge would be:
- ✓ *Understanding of the sales process*
- ✓ *Principles of accounting/ finance*
- ✓ *Understanding statements*
- ✓ *Principles of credit management- how bad debt occurs/ how to prevent*
- ✓ *Market/ economic trends*
- ✓ *Business problems/ needs*
- ✓ *Credit policies/ Legal aspects*

How effectively are you able to transfer this knowledge to the customer to enable him to part with the money owed to your company is a skill.
Now there are various types of skill sets that people possess- Some examples for skills are:
Negotiation skills
Selling skills (helpful for a collector!)
Telephone skills
Meticulous in documentation
Time management

Team Working
Presentation Skills
Ability to present in writing
Strategist- prepares and plans
Effective communication

But having Knowledge and Skills alone is not enough. There are many sales and collection personnel that have a great bank of knowledge along with the necessary skills, but yet have been total failures. Reason being they had a lousy attitude or very poor habits that killed a potential sale or the potential in them; that ultimately affected theirs and their organizations credibility
What you are seeing on the pie chart is the mental make-up of a Professional Debt Collector

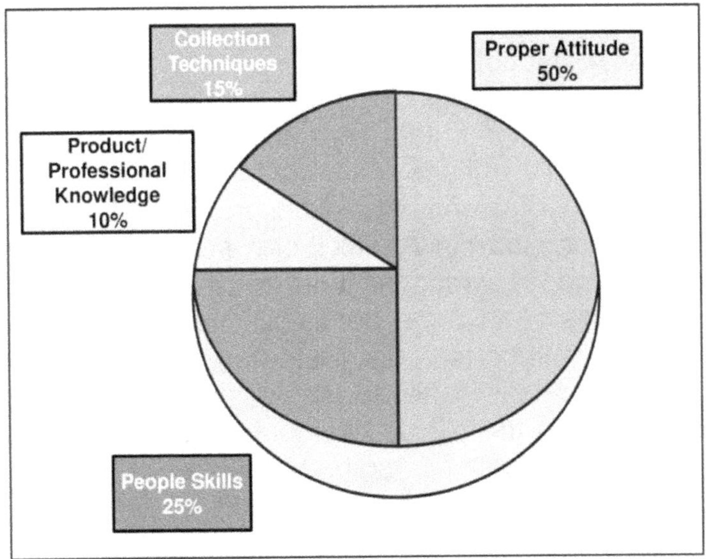

As you will see, 50% has to do with the Attitude, followed by 25% on People Skills. In other words, if you don't have the required knowledge or skills to service the customer, as you can see, you may be able to still succeed with the right attitude and people skills, because those two account for 75%. Now don't get me wrong, I am not saying that you should not work on your knowledge and skills…Absolutely no!

What I am saying is that given that you have the right attitude coupled with the right people skills, knowledge and collection techniques; you don't have to guess where your sales or your collection results would be!

Let us look at this a little differently….Assuming you have the right attitude and people skills, which together comprise of 75% but lack the required knowledge and skills, well then, to me, with the right attitude you can easily learn them. In any case knowledge and selling/ collection techniques are teachable, but not Attitude!

Attitude is the outlook or perception towards a given situation, and for a debt collector this is crucial and foundational! Attitude is made up from our upbringing, environment, exposure etc. It would therefore be extremely difficult or it would take a long time to undo a wrong attitude that has gone in all these years. And for a debt collection professional this is very important- as customers remember the wrong or negative attitude longer, and can use this as an excuse to hold up payment. You are the only thing the customer sometimes sees of your company- and this is the impression formed of your entire company- good or bad! It takes a long time to undo this negative feeling about your company in the mind of the customer.

And all this requires on-going: PRACTICE!
- ✓ **P**romptness: Prepared and swift to act.
- ✓ **R**eliability: Trusting or deserving of complete confidence.
- ✓ **A**ccuracy: The ability to observe and act with precision. Accuracy in documentation/ reports etc
- ✓ **C**ourtesy: The ability to be gracious, obliging and polite.
- ✓ **T**actfulness: The ability to say the right thing without offence, and knowing when to be firm.
- ✓ **I**nformation: Being equipped with all the required information and data.
- ✓ **C**ompetence: The ability and capacity to carry out a task on time/efficiently
- ✓ **E**mpathy: Emotional or intellectual identification with the other person.

At this stage it is important to realize that there are **3 A's of Business life**:

Ability, Ambition and **Attitude**

Ability establishes 'what' someone does
Ambition determines 'how much' he does
Attitude 'guarantees how' he does it!

Ability will bring one a pay cheque
Ambition will get him a raise
Attitude alone will lead to success in everything!

Attitude is actually the 'YOU on the job. When ability and ambition in two people are about equal, how does the boss select one over the other for promotion? Here is where attitude is the deciding factor. Attitude reflects a little plus- that something extra is given willingly though not required.

If you look at the word A-T-T-I-T-U-D-E itself, is it a mere coincidence that "I" comes first and "U" later? If this has any significance, then in trying to understand the attitudes of people, we should first examine ourselves in relation to other people!

Because attitude is so very important, this is why it is so crucial to fill our minds with the right positive thoughts because our thoughts work into decisions that form our actions and this continued action leads to a habit, which eventually makes up our attitude. Your habits today will become your attitude in the days to come. That's why it is important to check our habits as well. As an example: The habit of late-coming, if not nipped in the early stages can lead it to becoming an attitude, with everything that you undertake being late or delayed! And for a debt collector, this would mean missing a payment opportunity!

Here are some examples of positive or right attitude:
- ✓ *Belief*
- ✓ *Commitment*
- ✓ *Desire*
- ✓ *Ability to take failure in your stride & learn from it*
- ✓ *Persistent goals*
- ✓ *Self-Motivation*
- ✓ *Enthusiasm*
- ✓ *Purpose*
- ✓ *Self-discipline*
- ✓ *Confidence*
- ✓ *Creativity*
- ✓ *Empathy*
- ✓ *Go the extra mile*
- ✓ *Self-improvement*
- ✓ *Time organization*

✓ …and most of all the *PASSION!*

Remember: Changes are always: M.A.D.E…!!!
Developing the right sales and customer service attitudes is not something that happens to you-it is something you make happen…and like any change, it is not easy!
Here are some steps that can help:
M- Mental Pictures: Visualize who you are, what you want, how will you conduct and carry yourself
A- Affirmations: Add a new self-image by talking positively
D- Daily Successes: Build confidence everyday by looking at your positives rather than negatives
E- Environmental Influences: Surround yourself with positive influencers, read positive stuff, listen and watch positive information etc

You are what you think! To change any habits, you must first change any thoughts, feelings and values!
Changing Bad Habits into Good Ones!
STEP # 1: List your bad habits
STEP # 2: What were the original causes?
STEP # 3: What are the supporting causes?
STEP # 4: Determine a positive habit to replace the bad one.
STEP # 5: Think about the good habit, its benefits and results.
STEP # 6: Take action to develop this habit.
STEP # 7: Daily act upon this habit for reinforcement.
STEP # 8: Reward yourself by noting one of the benefits from your good habit
Here are some key characteristics and attributes of successful/ effective collectors:

- ✓ Highly positive attitude
- ✓ Outgoing, not introverted
- ✓ Good communicator (Ability to communicate clearly, using positive language- the right choice of words, as sometimes our words could get us into a problem or be used as an excuse!)
- ✓ Persistence/ tenacity (determined/ not giving up)
- ✓ Patience/ maintains composure
- ✓ Good listening skills
- ✓ Alert and attentive
- ✓ Time management and prioritizing
- ✓ Problem solver
- ✓ Always prepared, systematic and organized- does research
- ✓ Meticulous, especially in record keeping and maintaining of follow-ups
- ✓ Pro-active approach
- ✓ A team player
- ✓ Resilience-to handle criticism and negative feedback
- ✓ Understands how to overcome objections. (When debtors are delinquent it is only human for them to have a ton of excuses.)
- ✓ Adaptability/ flexibility
- ✓ Balances empathy with collections
- ✓ Assertive, not timid or aggressive
- ✓ Persuasive, not a 'take it or leave it' attitude
- ✓ Goal oriented/ focused
- ✓ Good negotiator
- ✓ Reasonable and yet firm, polite and courteous- Being able to do a balance, by being firm, while yet soft! An iron fist in a velvet glove!

- ✓ Manages emotions
- ✓ Enjoys achieving targets and deadlines

What makes a 'Recession-Ready' Collection Professional Different?

We've probably heard this saying: *"It's not what happens to you; it's how you handle it."* And I think during times like a business crisis, slump or downturn this is truer than ever.

A prolonged business or economic downturn can be demoralizing, and even frightening.

Research has found that mindset is 80 per cent of sales. When self-limiting beliefs, self-doubt, fear, or the inability to recover from rejection creeps into the mind of the salesperson it can significantly affect the sales effectiveness. If you don't believe in what you are selling, it will show out through you- through your very doubts in your own value proposition, the solution, the prices, or whether your company can deliver-by now lacking assertiveness, enabling the customer to begin to doubt you even more!

When business drops badly and nothing seems to work, it's easy for anyone to fall into the trap of doom-and-gloom thinking. And as the slump continues, one may even begin to panic or become depressed- typically like a deer paralyzed in front of headlights, aware of the danger but too frozen with fear to do anything about it. But on the contrary one would need to act to solve these problems. And for this to happen, the most important ingredient for a sales person at this crucial period is mental toughness- to remain strong in mind and spirit, to push through and reverse the downturn and restore business to profitability. The greatest danger is in doing nothing or, worse, giving up

When you are fighting your way out of a business downturn, it takes a lot of energy, time, and effort. Having a positive mental attitude gives you that mental energy to keep going even in the face of what seems to be apparent failure.

Having the Right Mindset and Attitude during an Economic Downturn. The Key Attributes!

Here are some key attributes found in 'Recession-ready' Sales and Collection Professionals:

- ✓ Optimism: Having optimism is a great asset as it helps the mind to look at every situation, positively, linking to the future, long term, open to new possibilities, and creating new realities- leaving you feeling less stressful
- ✓ Resilience: Those with strong mental resilience know very well that they can bounce back from any type of challenges that may come their way. This is a great attribute as, having a resilient mentality can remind one that obstacles, setbacks, and failures are just great learning tools to move forward and grow stronger.
- ✓ Analytical skills: It is the problem-solving skills- the ability to think clearly, staying "in the know", analyzing and assessing situations in the business, the market, etc and acting decisively on the findings, and further creating proactive strategies ahead of any major challenges, is another important attribute much needed.
- ✓ Flexibility: Being flexible allows one to be willing to compromise when facing difficulties, by listening to others- their concerns, needs, feedback and ideas and acting accordingly and recession times are when this attribute

will help immensely in making adjustments to steer forward.

- ✓ Resourcefulness: A recession may require a collection professional to be able to effectively use the available resources, time, creativity etc to maximize revenues coming in.
- ✓ Adaptive: The ability to adapt to ever-changing situations and scenarios will be very helpful as another attribute to enable the business become more recession-resistant. This could mean, sometimes just moving away from what is being done to move into uncharted areas- by being able to switch gears within the organization and identify ways to create a growing revenue stream despite an economic downturn
- ✓ Enthusiasm: It the fire or desire inside that will keep one going. Like the yeast in a cake- it rises to give its best!

Effective Collectors have **S.Y.S.T.E.M.S. And by doing so it...**

Saves
You
Stress
Time
Energy
Money &
Sleepless nights

To Sum up!

To be Successful as a Debt Collector one must have a combination of:

People Driven Skills *(Team player, Communicator etc)*

+

Process Driven Skills *(Systems, Procedures, Meticulous Recording and Reporting)*
with the
Right Attitude!

Finally, in closing this chapter, I would be failing if I did not let you into ONE KEY FACTOR, besides all the points provided so far, that can actually help to a great extent in ensuring your money comes in on time…and that is:

Collecting your Company's Money, is Everybody's Business!

Not just the sales guy, not only the collector, but right from the CEO to the very dispatch clerk- every single person has a role to play in ensuring that your money comes in on time. You could be wondering how a dispatch clerk could affect your collections from coming in. Well, if the invoice is locked in his cupboard or drawer and not dispatched at the right time, you have lost that time. I can provide examples how each position can in some way deter the money from coming in, if not the right way/ on time!

Steps to Professionally Collecting your Money!

There are three key steps to every collection call, irrespective of whether on phone or in person:
Pre –Call Planning
The Collection Call
Follow Up

Pre-Call Planning

If you want every call to be successful then a little bit of advance planning and ground work can help a lot. You cannot just pick up the phone or walk into a customer's place and ask for your payment, without checking and having all data right at your end. By preparing in advance, you have all the facts you need and are not likely to be caught, off guard or unawares by anything that the customer tells you. You will feel more confident and the call will go smoothly resulting in you meeting your objective.

Before we go any further into this, let us first ask: Why Prepare?
- ✓ *Makes you feel more confident*
- ✓ *You are able to discuss intelligently*
- ✓ *Saves time – yours and the customer*
- ✓ *Get to understand customer current situation*
- ✓ *Become more aware of business*
- ✓ *Your customers respect for you goes up*
- ✓ *Professional in the eyes of the customer*
- ✓ *Customer knows you have called to genuinely help*
- ✓ *You are proving that you are unlike other collectors*

- ✓ *And…The customer knows now that he cannot take you for a ride!*

Pre-call Planning
- ✓ Self-Mental/ Physical
- ✓ Ourselves: Look inwards first! Was it as per the terms/ Is it our fault?
- ✓ Customer: Intent and ability/ past records/ Right person
- ✓ An understanding of why customers don't pay
- ✓ Benefits (to this customer) of paying on time!
- ✓ Documents: Current and past transactions- carry copies!
- ✓ Check past efforts to collect: How, Who, When and What happened?
- ✓ Strategy: How are we going to approach?

Questions to ask at Pre-call Planning stage
- ✓ Who has defaulted in the agreement?
- ✓ Is your own company at fault?
- ✓ Were there previous collection efforts?
- ✓ Company records should indicate what letters, calls, or contacts were made
- ✓ What is the past payment record?
- ✓ Is the customer frequently overdue? How often?
- ✓ Is there a pattern to his delinquency? What is it?
- ✓ Who is the right person to talk to?
- ✓ What is the best payment plan to suggest?
- ✓ What are the best questions to ask to uncover reasons for delayed payment?
- ✓ What is the most appropriate initial approach to take- phone call, email, visit?

Evaluating Customers Intent and Ability

A Professional Collector must have the ability to accurately evaluate a customer's <u>intent</u> and <u>ability</u> to pay

Four questions must therefore be sought:
- ✓ What is the customer's intent to pay?
- ✓ What is the customer's ability to pay?
- ✓ What are the timescales over which the customer's intent and ability might change?
- ✓ What is the degree of likely change?

Unlike ability to pay, intent to pay has nothing to do with financial capability, but focuses solely on responsibility. The high intent customer accepts that the debt is something that should be repaid in full, and that they may need to consider reasonable lifestyle changes in order to repay the debt.

Keeping the Right Records before attempting your call

Checklist before writing / telephoning:
- ✓ Name / Address / Contact person
- ✓ Customers Reference/ Order number / Date / Etc
- ✓ Invoice number, Due date, Amount due
- ✓ Current and past records
- ✓ Assignment completion date / other instructions etc
- ✓ Updations of payments received if any / dates
- ✓ Updated statement of account

You are likely to land up with these responses if you are not prepared:
- ✓ Which invoice no. are you referring to?
- ✓ Are you sure the invoice was sent to this branch?

✓ I`m sure we paid you last week, check with your accounts department!
✓ You sent us a credit note which cleared our account
✓ Can you give me the invoice no?

Checklist to being better prepared-if on a premise (fact-to-face) call!
✓ Schedule of calls for the day (Territory Management- if premise call)
✓ Files/History case papers
✓ Documents pertaining to the accounts for the day
✓ Business cards/ID card
✓ Pens/ Note pad/ I-pad, Diary
✓ Anticipated questions/ concerns
✓ Role play/Rehearse your answers

Remember: *Effective collections do not just happen...They are the results of good planning!*

A Few Golden Rules to keep in mind on a Debt Collection Call:

- ✓ Avoid a casual salutation of *'Hi/ Hello'*- use a more professional one like a *'Good Morning/ Good Afternoon Mr....'* especially to new customers!
- ✓ If possible try to address them by their surname rather than 'first name', especially to new customers
- ✓ If you are on a premise call, avoid having any beverages or drinks offered to you by the customer. Think back; this has always diluted and deviated from the subject that you are present there for. Sometimes it's the debtor's tactic to do just that!
- ✓ Avoid *'How are you?' 'How's business?'* You are only asking for trouble. The response for *'How are you?'* from the customer would be something like: *'Oh, we had a sickness or death recently...all of our money was spent on that'.* And the response to *"How is business?"* would be something like: *"Very bad, this pandemic or economic crises all around has really hit us so badly"*
  You asked the wrong questions, so you get the wrong answers! Avoid these type of questions. That is why it is important to prepare the type of questions you want to ask the customer, at your pre-call planning stage itself.
  - ✓ Only one purpose: Focus on the objective of call: There are times when the customer

will sway away from the payment by tempting you with an order. Always get back, by thanking him, but appreciating that he clears this payment first.
- ✓ Watch body language (Customers and yours): Customer's: This can be a great indicator of whether he is trying to avoid you. Yours: Walk/talk with confidence. Remember it is your money- so do not feel bad or shy asking for it
- ✓ *'When can you make payment?'* Never ask this question, as you are putting the ball in the customers' court, and if he answers with a 'next year', you will not be able to do anything to get him to change that to the near future!
- ✓ *"I have a target! I am under pressure. I may lose my job"* (The customer actually doesn't care. You are only diminishing your position in front of him. You are the boss now- so act like one!)
- ✓ If you want to be treated with respect- Dress to get that respect!

The Collection Call

Given below are the Key Steps to a Professional Collection Call

- ✓ Introduction
- ✓ Reason for the call
- ✓ Deliberate pause
- ✓ Questions to uncover/ understand position
- ✓ Transition to payment plan
- ✓ The payment plan
- ✓ Overcoming objections
- ✓ Close and confirm

Let us deal with each of these steps now individually…

It is important to get started on the "right foot" with your customer. You will want to be confident and relaxed, while at the same time, conveying to the customer your seriousness about collecting your money and this can come from the right tone. Remember to sound pleasant and self-confident on the phone, as at the outset of the call itself, your voice must reflect your interest in getting the account resolved.

Introduction

Your introduction must consist of the following 4 steps:

- ✓ Salutation: Good Morning/ Good Afternoon (not a '*Hi*' or '*Hello*')
- ✓ Greet the customer, by using his or her correct name. Address individuals as '*Mr.*' *or* '*Ms.*', and try not to call them by their first name, especially for new customers.
- ✓ Identify yourself. Giving your own name helps personalize the call: '*My name is Sarah Jackson*'
- ✓ Identify your company. Identifying your company or organization helps legitimize the call: '*I am calling from ABC International, Delhi*'

Reason for the call

Give the purpose of your call. Let the customer know exactly why you are calling.

'The reason I'm calling you Mr. Customer is to let you know that there is an amount of 55555 pertaining to our invoice no.11, dated 15th September, which has been pending for over x days!' **Or** *'The reason I'm calling you Mr. Customer is to resolve your account,*

pertaining to our invoice no.11, dated 15th September for an amount of 55555, which is past due the date!'
Deliberate pause
This is a vital step. As soon as you've finished with the reason (mentioned above) just shut up! (Pause for a few seconds!) Human beings hate silence, so this pause gives the customer that chance to speak, during which time he would probably agree to the said amount and may provide a way of resolving the issue. But if he doesn't respond to this opportunity, you are ready to move to your next step
Questions to uncover/ understand position:
Three most important purposes of questioning
To gather information
To seek clarification
To establish commitment
Eg; (*'So are we agreeable then', 'So you will take care of that…'*)
Though there are several types of questions, for the purpose of this exercise let us look at just the 2 most important ones ie;
OPEN Questions
CLOSED Questions
Depending on what type of answer you want from the other person, either of these questions are used.
Eg; If I asked you: *'Did you have your dinner'?*
Or *'Do you like this training session?'* or *'Are you going home this evening'?*
The only possible answer that you could give me would either be a *'yes'* or a *'no'*
That is why this type of Question is called a 'closed Question', because the only possible answer would be a one word- with either a *'yes'* or *'no'*
Closed questions usually begin with:
'Are you…'

'Will you…'
'Do you…'
'Would you…'
They are usually not very helpful in starting a conversation and extracting information. However, most sales/ collection personnel are more comfortable asking such questions, which we need to avoid at this stage.

The opposite of 'closed' is the obvious: 'open'.
Open questions allow the customer to open up or do the talking and are used to encourage a client to speak freely about a concern or expand on something already raised during the conversation
Always remember this: Open Questions generally begin with 5W's and 1 H ie;
Who?
What?
When?
Where?
Why?
How?
If we were to redo that example again using open questions, they would go something like this: *'What did you have for dinner?' 'How do you feel about this training?' 'What plans do you have for this evening'?*
These questions will certainly not fetch you a *'yes'* or *'no'* like how closed questions do. But they would allow the other person to open up with information which is what you as a sales person/ collector would want.
So a good fact-finder is a searching open -end question which demands a detailed response. It requires more than a "yes" or "no". The purpose of a good fact-finding question is to get the customer to

state his <u>reason for not paying on time</u> and to help learn how to present (or modify) our payment plan to get his agreement.

The two criteria to be considered:

Is it open-end so that it allows the customers to do the talking?

Does it encourage the customer to explain why he hasn't paid?

Try not to use closed questions, as these will not enable you get information and make progress. You can very well guess the answers from the customer by asking such closed questions:

Examples of Close-Ended Questions to avoid!

Are you able to make payments?

Can you pay the balance in full?

Is there anyone who can assist?

Do you have the balance?

Can you talk to someone and see if they can help?

Are you able to send your payment this month?

Here are a few good examples of Open-Ended Questions

What happened to make your payment so late?

How can we help you to stay within the statement period?

What can we do to help you get your account current?

Listening Skills

While we are still on this fourth step of Questioning (to uncover/understand position), as the customer talks, you as a professional would need to listen attentively.

'People were designed with two ears and one mouth, and that is the ratio in which to use them'!

How to be a good listener?

One of the greatest skills that you as a Collector can develop is the skill of listening. The best Salespeople/ Collectors are the ones that do less talking and more of listening and that is why I believe God gave us two ears and one mouth- so we would do more listening than talking!

Here are some keys to be an "active" listener:

- ✓ Suspend judgment, initially- Keep an open mind
- ✓ Focus on the speaker and what he/she is saying
- ✓ Never interrupt while the customer speaks
- ✓ Tolerate silence. Silence can initially be uneasy, but if you practice tolerating it, you will find it very beneficial especially when negotiating.
- ✓ Listen for facts and key words
- ✓ Avoid distractions and never carry on side conversations
- ✓ Assess what you've heard
- ✓ Take notes of key points
- ✓ Clarify and reconfirm what the customer has told you- never assume!
- ✓ Never attempt doing anything else while on the phone with a customer! It's a big disturbance and bad manners

Before you respond, assess the information you heard by asking yourself four questions in your mind:

- ✓ *What has the customer told me?*
- ✓ *What can I do with this information?*
- ✓ *What else do I need to know?*
- ✓ *What questions do I still need to ask?*

To show you're listening actively:

✓ Respond by using terms like, *'Go on', Uh huh'* and *'mmm'*
✓ Stay always tuned in an alert
✓ To show that you have, understood:
  Use, phrases like *"I see," "I understand"*
✓ Paraphrase, *"So you want me to …"*

Transition to payment plan

Now that you know or have an idea of the customer's situation, you will need to bring him back to a payment plan as quickly as possible. The best way to do this is with a transition statement_that links your solution with a desire the customer had just mentioned to you. An example is:

'Mr. Raj, you said you wish there was some way to take care of this…and I think I've got just the right plan that will enable you to do that.'

Now, even if the customer hasn't expressed such a desire, you can still focus his or her attention on the plan, by saying something like:

'Mr. Raj, I've been working on a plan to get your account up to date, and here is a way that we could do it.'

The customer must eventually feel that you genuinely have understood his situation and that you are eagerly interested in resolving it- and this can come greatly from the tone of your voice

Overcoming Objections

An important component at this stage (or can happen earlier too) is the handling of objections.

During the sales/ collection process, even the best salespeople/ collectors can encounter objections that are difficult to handle. An objection is a concern or question raised by the client that delays or prevents you from proceeding to the next step. It is usually a stalling technique or postponement. But by using the right techniques, however, you can handle these objections without losing your focus.

To overcome an objection:

- ✓ You first acknowledge it.
- ✓ Then question to determine what specifically the customer is objecting to.
- ✓ Get agreement on the parts of the plan he is not objecting to.
- ✓ Work out an agreeable solution to the part he objects to.
- ✓ Anticipation and being prepared helps! And one way to do that is to: Identify the various objections that you encounter-Make a list of debtor stalls
- ✓ Stress on the 'Benefits to the customer by paying you on time' (covered in an earlier chapter)
- ✓ Learn to master your list
- ✓ Believe in yourself

Here is a list of some of the top 12 'Most Common Customer Excuses/ Objections' (With suggested responses)

Customer Excuse 1: Lost the invoice / require a duplicate

Background to Excuse: Important to find out why further documentation is necessary. How was the invoice lost? Ask-open-ended questions.

Suggested Response: Yes certainly, but may I ask why a duplicate is necessary?

May I confirm that you have received the goods delivered in April at your factory located at ABC

Location and that Rupees X is now overdue by Y weeks? To prevent any further delay where and to whom should we address the duplicate invoice and soon after which can we expect to receive this due at our office please?

Customer Excuse 2: The Person who signs the cheque is away from the office/ No body available to sign the cheque.

Background to Excuse: This is a very common excuse and is used often as a delaying tactic. Try to check if there is an alternative authority. Go for a promise of settlement with a definite date for action and call back. Lastly request for payment to be made online

Suggested Response: It must be really difficult, but how long is he going to be away? Who is dealing with his work during this time? How are other essential payments being made during his absence? Can we discuss the best way to resolve this situation in Mr. X's absence please? I'm sure your office could look at an online transfer considering that the payment is long overdue already.

Customer Excuse 3: No Money

Background to Excuse: Since the customer has tried this in the past and got away with it, he will now use this excuse often. You will need to probe or do a little bit of investigation among staff or others to assess if it is a genuine cash flow problem or could it be a more serious symptom of bankruptcy.

The last resort would be to ask them to return the goods supplied.

Suggested Response: Our records show that you have for most times paid regularly on time. Could you explain what the situation is now that prevents you from settling as usual?

May I just reconfirm that you have had our service to the value of Rs. X during the month of April and our invoice has been pending since then? When do you see this situation getting resolved? Not having sufficient funds to settle our account is difficult for both of us. We may have to make arrangements to recall our goods if we are not able to see any positive signs soon.

Customer Excuse 4: Waiting for our customers to pay us

Background to Excuse: This is a common excuse but an agreeable date must be reached as to when the due payment will be sent. Communicate politely yet strongly that the transaction is between us and them- the buyer. We are not bankers to fund their business.

We may need to offer a final threat, of 'stop supply' and or recall our goods supplied if this continues or persists. He needs to realize that you are one company he cannot delay payment with in the future!

Suggested Response: I can appreciate that cash flow is extremely important (particularly as you are a 'small' company) and that can be very annoying if customers do not settle invoices promptly. As you can see, we are of course in the same situation and wish to therefore confirm with you our terms agreed upon, where we expect payment within X weeks.

This Rs. Y is now overdue by Z weeks (months!) and we are looking for complete settlement immediately or else much against our wishes, we may have to make arrangements to recall our goods if we are not able to see any positive signs soon.

Customer Excuse 5: Wrong price mentioned.
Background to Excuse: Could be genuinely our fault. Check details at our end. If we are at fault rectify immediately.
Suggested Response: I can understand that you would not be prepared to pay for goods that are not rightly priced. As you say that we have not mentioned the right prices on this occasion, we can right away do the changes over email, with a follow up by courier, so that there need be no further delay in settlement. Can we agree that the right prices are Rs. X for goods delivered in March?

Customer Excuse 6: Faulty/damaged goods delivered.
Background to Excuse: Check to see the authenticity of this claim. Ask for photo shot of the damaged goods. If real, assist in sorting out from our end. If it appears to be an excuse and no proof provided of such damage, go for payment in full.
Suggested Response: I can understand that you would not be prepared to pay for goods that are not working as expected. How many items are you referring to? Can we have photo shots of these damaged goods, for our records and future references? (If quantity or numbers are small, then suggest the following...) This represents a small part of the overall total of the Rs .X overdue. If we take off or lessen Rs. Y pertaining to these damaged goods, then can we expect the settlement of the balance of Rs. X-Y immediately please?

Customer Excuse 7: Re-structuring within the company (or takeover).

Background to Excuse: Likely to be an excuse because of the internal confusion which often causes problems and hiccups in procedures. Probe how other statutory payments are being made during this time. Try moving them away from these excuses to a positive discussion for full settlement – Ask for a post dated cheque if need be! Finally, you may need to caution them that any further supplies may be delayed till existing outstanding dues are cleared

Suggested Response: Yes it could certainly be disruptive having a re-structure (takeover) take place, with all departments affected and going through this. How long do you think this would take? ? How are other essential payments being made during this period?

I'm sure your office could look at an online transfer or providing a post-dated cheque, considering that the payment is long overdue already. May we just re-confirm that you have received our goods to the value of Rs. X during the month of April? And to fulfill our terms we would need your full remittance to this value immediately.

Customer Excuse 8: 'Cheque in the post/courier' or payment has already been made.

Background to Excuse: Could be true; and if so, the customer will appreciate you probing further for the said details. If not true – then first request them to recheck at their end once again. Sometimes the dispatch section could be sleeping over the courier. When you don't just take this excuse lightly by believing in him right away, he will recognize your thoroughness and will think twice about using the excuse again. If no cheque is received in a few days, a further call is required to pursue and may be threaten

Suggested Response: Good, thank you, In order to make sure that it has not gone astray and so that I can progress it at this end, could I ask you to tell me the date it was sent, the amount, the cheque number, to which address and to whom was it posted/couriered to? (Ask for document number if by courier…to trace!)

Customer Excuse 9: Our organization is going into liquidation

Background to Excuse: Need to probe or do a little bit of investigation among staff or others to assess if it is genuine. Check status of account and likelihood of settlement, even if in parts/ installments or to issue a post-dated cheque. If all fails, ask them to return the goods supplied.

Suggested Response: We are as anxious as you to settle the situation as it stands with our company, as; not having sufficient funds to settle our account is difficult for both of us. So can we go through the details of the statement of account and work out the best way of ensuring our needs (demands) are met based on our business terms? May I just reconfirm that you have had our service to the value of Rs. X during the month of April and our invoice has been pending since then? Can we suggest that you make part payments (or one post dated cheque for full amount) that will help ease your situation, while getting this outstanding cleared?

We may have to make arrangements to recall our goods if we are not able to see any positive signs soon.

Customer Excuse 10: Changing our banks

Background to Excuse: If it the first time (one time problem) and genuine from a good customer, then allow a week for solution. Acknowledge the situation and show interest and concern. If you know it is an excuse (after probing) settlement must be made

Suggested Response: Changing of banks, these days, do not normally cause much delays, as the procedures are generally instant and straightforward. I would like to just reconfirm that you have had the goods delivered to the value of Rs. X and that this balance has now been outstanding for Y weeks.

May I ask, with which bank will you be operating with from now on (branch and from which date)? As soon as that happens, may I ask that you arrange for an online transfer of this amount to avoid any further delays?

Customer Excuse 11: Cheque sent, but with no signature

Background to Excuse: Acknowledge and thank them for this. Chances are that it may have been an oversight. But most often this practice is used as a delaying tactic. Request for online payment, while holding to this unsigned cheque till the payment is received.

Suggested Response: Thank you for the cheque to the value of Rs .X on 30th April.

Unfortunately, were you aware that the cheque that you sent had no signature? I am sure it must have been an oversight and so in order to avoid any further delays, may we now request you to arrange for an online transfer for the amount due?

Customer Excuse 12: Our order no. is not on your invoice.

Background to Excuse: If our mistake, it has to be rectified and with a system to avoid future recurrence. Immediately provide the customer an order no. and continue to go for full settlement by agreeing a date when to expect full remittance preferably by online transfer.

Suggested Response: We usually add order numbers on all our invoices, but as you say that we have not included one on this occasion we are allocating a number right now over the phone, with a follow up by email so that there need be no further delay in settlement, requesting you to process this immediately for settlement please. Can we agree the figure shown on this invoice is Rs. X for goods delivered in March?

Handling the E Category Customer

When we were on the subject of categorizing customers in one of the earlier chapters, we looked at the last Category-E: *'Do what you want-I will not pay'*.

Fortunately with the advent of the 'Insolvency and Bankruptcy Code (IBC)' in recent years, this has now given the collector another powerful tool especially for such E category customers-to bring these incorrigible and recalcitrant customers to book. However, this being a code which has some rules, regulations and legal formalities to comply with, before somebody takes recourse to it, has not been dealt with in a detailed manner. It was thought that dealing with IBC (which entails adhering to rules and regulations and legal matters) in a detailed manner will only detract from the main purpose of this book, which is to collect the money, whilst still keeping the customer.

Key steps to handling complaints:
- ✓ **Thank the customer:** The fact that the customer has come or called to complain, means that they are giving your organization a chance to rectify things. You have another opportunity to turn this customer as a well-wisher. He could have gone away quietly- but he has given your organization another chance- grab it and use it to turn the customer around.
- ✓ **Listen and stay calm**: Aim to diffuse the customer's feelings and clarify the exact nature of the problem.
- ✓ **Don't justify, argue, make excuses, interrupt or pass the buck**: Just stick to the facts, keep off what happened in the past and focus on what is going to happen now.
- ✓ **Sympathize:** This means sympathizing with the fact that the person has a problem, not accepting any blame as you are currently hearing only one side of the story (theirs).
- ✓ **Ask probing questions to verify facts:** This will give you more detailed information about the specific complaint and allow you to see a way through to a possible solution to the problem
- ✓ **Check back your understanding:** Reconfirm or paraphrase what you heard.
- ✓ **Agree a course of action and timeframe**: It is essential to find a solution which is satisfactory for the customer and from your organization's point of view.

- ✓ **Check that the course of action is carried out:** If you agree with the customer that something will happen by a certain date, you must check that it has in fact happened. If it hasn't, you must take action to avoid making the problem even more serious.
- ✓ **Check for the satisfaction of the customer**
- ✓ **Thank the customer again**
- ✓ **Work on setting your system** in order to ensure such mistakes or lapses are not repeated

Turn Negative to Positive!
Some useful phrases you can use:
> *"I'll be glad to…"*
> *"What would you consider right or fair?"*
> *"I'm sorry you feel that way"*
> *"Would you be willing to…?"*
> *"Thank you for drawing this to my attention."*

How to deal with IRATE Customers
- ✓ Give the customer space to let off steam before you try to steer them towards a discussion
- ✓ Don't take it personally, and always be calm
- ✓ If the customer is abusive and you can't steer the conversation onto how you can solve the problem, seek help from your supervisor
- ✓ If the customer won't calm down and they've caught you unprepared, agree to look into the problem and tell them when you'll call or e-mail them

Always remember that: An Angry Customer…
May have 4 F's that could be bothering them!
Fitness: They may have a health problem

Family: They may have a spouse/ children/ other family problem
Finance: They may have a money problem
Firm: They may have a job problem (boss/colleague/ other)
And they may just be taking that out on you!
Take it seriously – <u>not</u> personally.

Steps to handle an Angry Customer

Dealing with an angry customer is an opportunity to learn, and an opportunity to turn a negative situation into a positive customer experience. How you react to an angry customer can make or break the perception the customer has about your organization.

Instead of backing away or avoiding an angry customer, use this opportunity to improve your product or service, and to work on building a better relationship with your customer. This is a great opportunity you have to solidify your relationship.

Here are a few key steps to keep in mind by taking responsibility when dealing with irate or dissatisfied customers – and turning them around to be your mouthpiece and ambassadors for your organization.

- ✓ Listen all the way out. Make sure the customer has told you everything. Don't interrupt.
- ✓ Ask open questions to understand their problem better, and to find out what it will take to help them – the way they want to be helped.
- ✓ Tell them you understand how they feel (This is powerful- try it!)
- ✓ Empathize with them. (Cite a similar incident or tell them that it makes you upset too)

Empathy doesn't necessarily mean agreeing with the customer. It means you truly understand how they feel. Comfort them.

✓ Maintain a calm tone of voice all through the conversation

✓ Use the customer's name in your conversation

✓ Agree with them, if at all possible. (Never argue or get angry.)

✓ Take notes and confirm back that everything has been covered, and they have said all they want/need to say.

✓ Be an ambassador for your company. Tell the customer you will personally handle it

✓ Don't blame others or look for a scope goat. Admit you (and or your organization) were wrong and take responsibility for correcting it.

✓ Apologize for the problem they're having. Acknowledging the mistake and letting the customer know you're really sorry will go a long way. Be thorough in your apology.

✓ Don't pass the buck. *"It's not my job."…"I thought she said this…" "He's not there right now."…* or *"Someone else handles that,"* are responses that are never right or acceptable to the customer.

✓ Avoid negative speech- Tell them what you can do, not what you cannot!

✓ Don't take it personally- but do take it seriously

✓ Respond immediately. When something goes wrong, people want (and expect) it to be fixed immediately. The customer wants it now- not at your time. Don't we all want it that way when we are customers ourselves!

- ✓ Find some common ground other than the problem. (Try to establish some rapport.)
- ✓ If you have the gift for humor, use it if possible. It is a very powerful tool as making people laugh puts them at ease.
- ✓ Work out all possible solutions, communicate, and agree upon the best solution. Give the customer choices if possible.
- ✓ Follow this up by confirming in writing if necessary. Tell them what you plan to do… and DO IT!
- ✓ Make a follow-up call after the situation is resolved. Check to see if they are totally satisfied
- ✓ Get a letter if you can. Resolving a problem in a favorable and positive way strengthens respect, builds character, and establishes a solid base for long-term relationships. Tell the customer you would appreciate a sentence or two about how the situation was resolved.
- ✓ Ask yourself: "What have I learned, and what can I do to prevent this situation from happening again? Do I need to make any changes?" Where?

Key advice- before the Final Step!

Before we move to the final step in this call, there is one important aspect that every collector must ensure and that is to take notes as well as to keep summarizing the discussions

Taking Notes

A professional collector will always take notes of key points and never depend on memory.

Before you even start on the fourth step- (the Questioning stage); you may like to indicate to the customer that you are taking notes: *'Is it okay Mr. Customer, if I jot down a few notes as we go along'*
By asking to take notes and doing so- even if the customer can't see you (if on phone), you are subtly indicating to the customer:
- ✓ *I care about your business*
- ✓ *I do not want to miss anything*
- ✓ *The competition may have called you and sounded aggressive and pushy, but - I am here to genuinely help!*
- ✓ *I am a professional*
- ✓ *And most importantly, by drawing his attention that you are noting whatever is being discussed, this would make him alert and more cautious from now on, especially when it comes to playing up with you!*

Clarifying and Reconfirming with Closed Questions and close the call

This is the time when closed questions are very useful. To clarify and reconfirm, restate in your own words what the client has said and ask him to verify your understanding. An example would be: *'Mr. Customer, Let me just take a minute to summarize, just to ensure that I've got the right information…You were mentioning that you would be making a payment of…. by tomorrow, the (20th of Nov)…Am I right Mr. So & So?'*

Why summarize?
- ✓ *It keeps complexities under control*
- ✓ *It tests progress*

- ✓ *It lets you restate what the other party has said*
- ✓ *It can help gain the initiative*
- ✓ *It can keep the discussion on track*
- ✓ *It can prevent misinterpretation, misunderstanding and subsequent bitterness*
- ✓ *In other words, summarizing helps you stay on top (but you take the point).*

By summarizing, you are making sure you have the right information and that you haven't left out anything.

Once you have secured the customers agreement on the payment plan, and re-confirmed the commitment to the payment arrangement, you can now end the call by thanking the customer for his or her commitment.

Finally, leave the customer with a good feeling, by ensuring you close in a positive, friendly and professional way

Key Factors for a Professional Collector to enable you stand out

Successful telephone collection is achieved through proper preparation prior to the telephone call, and more importantly, being in control of the call. Three areas are vital for you to have control over:

1. Yourself   2. The Debtor   3. Your Conversation

When you call a customer, you must ensure the following:
- ✓ Always tell the truth! Be honest -it really is the best approach. You WILL get found out if you lie. If you do not know something admit it with the assurance that you would get back with the answer. And do so as committed! Using methods that are honest and forthright is what separates a professional from the rest.
- ✓ Wear some armor-Process of collection isn't easy. You need to build some resilience to rejection. If you don't, it will be a task that becomes increasingly scary. It isn't for the faint hearted. Constantly find ways to keep yourself charged up.
- ✓ Your attitude determines your altitude! Always have a positive attitude.
- ✓ Begin each shift with a positive attitude and try your best to maintain that attitude throughout the day – even if you get discouraged. Prospects will notice a negative tone in your

voice. A positive and upbeat tone, however, can be contagious

✓ Smile-It transmits to your voice. Your customer can actually feel it
✓ Have your list in front of you before calling
✓ For each of the customers have the complete account details along with respective documentation in front of you. In case of a disputed account, update yourself with feedback from the other concerned departments and be ready to handle all possible objections
✓ Be sure of the name, designation of the key person you are going to call
✓ Have sufficient stationery ready in front of you- pens, pencils, calendar, diary etc
✓ Know exactly what you are going to say. If possible keep points
✓ Rehearse your flow of what you plan to say before each call.
✓ Follow the steps outlined earlier to ensure you have a control over the call
✓ Posture/ Body language (Sit up erect- you begin to feel more confident)
✓ Try standing up when talking to a debtor- for a feeling of increased control
✓ Managing vocal qualities-Rate of speech
                                              -Volume
                                              -Tone
                                              -Word choice
✓ Beware of the wrong tone of voice: Because the person to whom you are speaking cannot see you, the telephone focuses full attention on the tone of your voice.

- ✓ Use the right rate of speech: The telephone exaggerates your rate of speech. If you speak too rapidly, it is hard for the other person to understand what you are saying. This, in turn, can lead to mistrust. On the other hand, speaking too slowly can lead to impatience or may sound boring to the listener. The average rate of speech is 150 words per minute. Find a 750 word article or speech. Read it aloud as you time yourself. You should read the message in exactly five minutes. Continue to practice until you can do it consistently, without fluctuating more than 10% either way.
- ✓ Always be courteous but assertive and professional
- ✓ Make sure you are talking to the key person who can give you what you want
- ✓ Telephone during "up" time - Best times are 9 AM to Noon; 2 PM to 4 PM; Never on Monday mornings or Friday afternoons. Never on Sundays or holidays.
- ✓ Block Your Time - Make or return phone calls at precisely the exact time you committed to. Don't even be 2-3 minutes late!
- ✓ Don't dwell on small talk: Small talk at the beginning of each call might seem friendly and natural. But too much of it can be distracting and time wasting.
- ✓ Predetermine how to maximize the value of every call. Before you speak to a prospect, have a game plan for all possibilities… if plan "A" doesn't work, you should be able to roll to plan "B" and "C" if necessary.
- ✓ Use of customer's name!
- ✓ Introduce yourself clearly

- ✓ Never ask: *'How are you are today'* or *'how is business?'* - It is a tell-tale sign of a typical sales call, and you are asking for trouble!
- ✓ Always state clearly why you are calling, "unpaid invoice number..."
- ✓ Ask good questions and avoid interruptions
- ✓ Practice being an effective listener
- ✓ Don't get distracted by ANYTHING else whilst on a call
- ✓ Be aware of your emotions as well as acknowledge the emotions of your customer
- ✓ Remember it is a business transaction. Hence avoid personal emotions in conversation.
- ✓ Ask them if the payment will be sent immediately
- ✓ If payment cannot be promised, ask why (do not interrupt)
- ✓ Provide a solution: never ask them what they can pay, and when
- ✓ Provide them with a second solution: if first solution is not possible
- ✓ If second solution is not taken, ask, "out of interest, what can you do?"
- ✓ Either accept or do not accept their offer
- ✓ Re-confirm understanding
- ✓ Accept: summarize the agreement, and what will happen if they default
- ✓ Always close the call with an assurance from the customer of a specific date for payment
- ✓ Send a confirmation letter, whether you accept or reject
- ✓ Record/ make notes of everything discussed during the call
- ✓ Update in your calendars/ system the follow-up action

- ✓ Always follow-up! Never give up. If the customer fails to call back, remember, that they could be just caught up with other things. Persistence matters from your end!
- ✓ Be Diligent: You want to make sure that each day is better than the previous day, in terms of number of calls, quality of calls, your updating of call register etc
- ✓ Always keep records of every call, even of the minutest conversations
- ✓ Role-play or record your calls to see what could have been done better. Listen back to improve your techniques. Make a record of what you've learnt from every call and improvise as you go forward.
- ✓ Finally…Proactive Collectors know that:
  - *If you don't ask, you don't get;*
  - *The sooner ask, the sooner you get;*
  - *The more you ask, the more you get;*
  - *A phone call gets before a letter gets;*
  - *Prime business calling times are10-12, 2.30- 4.30 and get a higher success rate;*
  - *Calling large accounts in the first week of each month allows time to sort out*
  - *blockages before month end;*
  - *Mentioning bills approaching due date never offends*

Monitoring Your Debts

What can prevent you from collecting your outstanding debts effectively? Here are some areas to check (red flags!)

Internal Factors (our office): Systems, Policies, Procedures, People, Training, Mindset, Improper Follow-up/Documentation, Assertiveness, etc
External Factors (Your Customers): Market, Competition, Environment, Promises made by Sales personnel, Can pay when I want attitude etc

Internal (At your set-up)
- ✓ Lack of proper procedures and systems (improper records/lack computers etc)
- ✓ Improper/ Inconsistent follow-up
- ✓ Test certificates not provided on time
- ✓ Partial shipments
- ✓ CGST/ SGST/ IGST difference
- ✓ Wrong supplies/ Wrong identifications
- ✓ Pushed with too much stocks (greater than their capacity)
- ✓ Too close a relationship (difficult asking for payment)
- ✓ False commitment
- ✓ Wrong billing
- ✓ Professional/Assertive approach needed
- ✓ Lack of or inadequate communication (Credit issues/Terms etc)
- ✓ Pressure for new/more business
- ✓ Resignation of collection person abruptly (continuity lost)

  ✓ Fear of competition (We may lose if we
    remind)

External (Your customers')
  ✓ Compares 'schemes/ credit periods' of the
    competition
  ✓ Fear of competitor
  ✓ General customer excuses for stalling (see
    separate chapter on objections)
  ✓ Inefficiency in their set-up
  ✓ Says somebody else placed order
  ✓ Lack of or inadequate communication
    (scheme/pricing/credit issues)
  ✓ Attitude of: Can move to another provider
  ✓ Can pay when I want (Intentional
    postponement of payment)
  ✓ Problem in billing
  ✓ Bill not received/lost
  ✓ Disagreement over the original agreement

**Using 'The Pareto Analysis' to monitor your
collections**

The 'Pareto Principle', was formulated after an
esteemed economist Vilfredo Pareto, and is also
known as the '80/20 rule'. The Pareto Analysis can
be very effective in managing and handling your key
debtors.

Basing your planning on this Pareto principle, will
help a lot in achieving your collection objectives by:
  ✓ Enabling you to cover-up or handle maximum,
    if not all of the overdue accounts
  ✓ Enabling you collect maximum cash to meet
    the target for the period
  ✓ Helping reduce the over dues to a minimum,
    with particular emphasis on the high risk ones.

What is the Pareto Principle? Pareto stated that: *'In any series of elements to be controlled, a selected small fraction in terms of number of elements almost always accounts for a large fraction in terms of effect'.* The Pareto Principle states that 80% of consequences come from 20% of the causes.

The principle comes to be known as the 80:20 rule, and is applicable in many situations:

80% of late deliveries will be caused by 20% of suppliers.

80% of complaints will be received from 20% of customers.

The general rule in business is that 80% of your sales will come from 20% of your customers. In the alternative, 20% of your business will come from 80% of your customers.

In our case, 20% of Customers will account for 80% of the receivables.

The 80:20 rule when applied to cash flow means that a small number of customers will be responsible for most of the debt problem. Most of your probable risk is with a small element of your customers. The solution is to at least vet this element regularly: it is unlikely that any one customer in the 80% of customer's category could cause you a financial crisis. But, the failure of one major customer would have a serious effect on profits and liquidity. Also, since most of the problem will be caused by only a small percentage of the customers, valuable time and effort should be concentrated on this small percentage. Again as a reminder, any portion of debt not collected, erodes the profit margin.

Days Sales Outstanding (DSO)
The common measurement for a company's collection ability is the ratio of debtors to turnover. Day's sales outstanding (DSO) is a measure of the average number of days that it takes a company to collect payment for a sale. DSO is often determined on a monthly, quarterly, or annual basis.
The days sales outstanding formula is as follows: Divide the total number of accounts receivable during a given period by the total value of credit sales during the same period and multiply the result by the number of days in the period being measured.

A simple system to calculate the money owed to you at any time, by which we can measure collections, is by working out how much of the previous month's money is still outstanding. If we set a target DSO, we can measure our progress on a regular basis.
The calculation consists of dividing the current credit balance by the annual credit sales turnover and multiplying by 365.

DAYS SALES OUTSTANDING- DSO

$$DSO = \frac{\text{Current Credit Outstanding}}{\text{Credit Sales Turnover}} \times 365$$

If an organizations' turnover is 12, 00, 000 on credit and its present outstanding balance is 197,620, then it's DSO=60, ie; it takes 60 days on an average to collect the money due to it

Another (most common) Method-Count Back Method

Another most common way is the 'count back' method. This is the best method of calculating DSO because the latest sales figures, which are most closely related to the Debtor's ledger balances, are used in the calculation. The method operates in the following manner.

a) If the balance in the relevant Debtor's Account is lesser than the sales of the latest month , the DSO is computed by converting the Debtor's balance as no of days sale of that latest month (Debtor's balance / average sales per day of the latest month)

b) If the balance in the relevant Debtor's Account is more than the latest month's sales it means the DSO is straightaway 30 plus and the procedure enumerated in the subsequent steps should be followed.

c) If the balance in the relevant Debtor's Account is more than the latest month's sales, the current month sales are deducted from the Debtor ledger balance as at the end of the relevant month. If this does not clear the debtor's balance in full, sales of the immediately preceding month are deducted. For each month of full deduction the DSO would be 30 days.

d) This exercise is repeated till such time the balance in the Debtor's Account is less than the sale of the month. Once that point is reached the remaining balance in the Debtor's Account is converted as the no of days' sale of that month (the earliest month) ie the remaining Debtor balance / average sales per day of the earliest month.

e) The sum total of the days in c and d would give us the DSO in terms of days in such cases.

The following example would explain the calculation of DSO.

DAYS SALES OUTSTANDING- DSO

Debtors, ending April 4,60,000- using a 30 day month

Month	Sales	D.S.O.	Count Back
Debtors	-	-	4, 60, 000
April	2, 00, 000	30/30	2, 60, 000
March	2, 30, 000	30/30	30, 000
February	2, 10, 000	4/30	-
Total	-	64 DSO	-

Note: The figure 460,000 is an assumed amount of total debt at this stage. The figure of **30**/30 is achieved when a **full** month's sales can be deducted from the debtor balance, as with April and March above. To achieve the figure of **4**/30: divide the February Sales (210,000) by 30 (the days in the month), to give you 7,000. Take the difference of the cumulative figure of March (430,000) from the debtor total (460,000) to give you 30,000. Divide the 30,000 by the 7,000 to give you **4** (4.28 to be exact). Thus the total DSO is 64 in this case.

If in the above example the Debtor balance as at the end of April is say 120000 (which is lesser than the sale of April) the DSO would be 120000/ average sales per day in April which would work out to 18 . The method is called 'count back' as we go from the latest month to the earlier months.

Exercise

To help you understand this more, can you now work out the DSO in the following two examples. (Solutions are provided at the end)

Count back Method- Example-1

Ledger balance is	30,000
September Gross Sales were are 30 days in September	12,000 – there
August gross sales were are 31 days in August	11,000 – there
July gross sales were are 31 days in July	14,000 – there

Count back Method- Example 2

Sales Ledger Balance - June 30 days	1,450,000	30
June Sales	650,000	
May Sales days	490,000	31
April Sales days	600,000	16

Now check your workings: Solutions to the Exercise above
Count back Method- Example-1

You take the balance on your debtor's ledger and subtract the current months gross sales and keep going back each month until the remainder gets to zero as follows:

Ledger balance is	30,000	
September Gross Sales were	12,000 – there	
are 30 days in September		
The balance remaining is	18,000	
August gross sales were	11,000 – there	
are 31 days in August		
The balance remaining is	7,000	
July gross sales were	14,000 – there	
are 31 days in July		

From the above figures the 30,000 balance represents all of September sales (=30 days), all of august sales (=31 days) and half July sales (= 15.5 days) So the DSO for this company for September is 30+31+15.5 which is **76.5 days**. The plus point of this method is that if the sales team had a bumper month and sold 24,000 – the ledger balance would increase to 42,000 – using the calculation above it would still come out at **76.5 days.**
Then every month you can track your progress as long as you get accurate gross sales figures, treat your cash sales consistently and make sure you have the same cut off point every month.

Count back Method- Example 2

Sales Ledger Balance - June 30	1,450,000	30 days
June Sales	650,000	
	800,000	
May Sales	490,000	31 days
	310,000	
April Sales = 600,000	310,000	16 days

No. of days in April x Balance/April Sales
30 x 310,000/600,000
DSO = 76.
A good DSO figure is one that is considered good for your industry. Some industries have 60, 90 or even 120 day's payment terms. The following is a guide if you <u>use 30 days</u> as a payment term.

DAYS SALES OUTSTANDING- DSO

The following is a guide if you <u>use 30 days</u> as a payment term

Very Good	Good	Fair	Poor
Under 45 Days	46-59	60-74	Over 75 Days

Aged Debt Analysis (by Category)
Knowing 'who owes you' is not as important as knowing 'when it was owed'.

AGED DEBT ANALYSIS
By Category

Knowing 'who owes you' is not as important as knowing 'when it was owed'

Priority 1	0-30 Days	Over 100000
Priority 2	31-90 Days	Over 200000
Priority 3	0-30 Days	Under 100000
Priority 4	31-90 Days	Under 200000
Priority 5	91+ Days	All

Call Reports for Debt Collections

The sample 'Call Reports' shown here are templates that are meant to be used on your computer to enable you be more effective in handling your day, your customers and managing your time, whilst keeping total control of your debtors:

Telephone Daily Activity Report

This will provide you a complete report and status of the calls made by your Collector/ You for each given day

TELEPHONE DAILY ACTIVITY SHEET

Outgoing Call Record Name: Date:

No of Calls	Company Name	Name & Title of Decision Maker	Date & Value of Last Payment	Outstanding Balance	Payment Secured	Promised Date

Daily Collection Report

This again provides by day the calls made by a collector, from the start to end of day along with status, and targets achieved each day.

DAILY COLLECTION REPORT

Location:........................
Name of Collector:...........
Check-out Time:..............
Check-in Time:................

Date:

Name of Account	Name & Title of Decision Maker	Tel . No/ Area Code	Time Called/ Visited	Nature of Call Premise/ Tele-call	No of Visits	Result/ Remarks

DAILY CN: BRTFWD CN :   CRFD CN:
 CQ: CQ: CQ: Manager's Signature

Daily Collection Call Report- By Customer

The 'Collection Call Report-By Customer' can be used for each customer- indicating the entire details of transactions

COLLECTION CALL REPORT- BY CUSTOMER

Customer Name:........................   Customer Code:...............
Telephone No:...........................   Order/ Contract No:...........
Invoice No:................................   Collector:.......................
Outstanding Amount:..................
Due Date:...................................

S. No	Date	Person Contacted/ Name/Title	REMARKS

The Follow-Up
This is the next step after you've obtained the customer's agreement-A dedicated and persistent follow-up!
Here are a few things that you must do:
Record your notes -diary/record on computer, log of calls, letters, phone calls, visits, etc
Update your records daily with all information- Someone taking over this account from you as collector should not have any difficulty
Take Action on the dates mentioned. Do not delay or postpone. If the customer knows that you can put up with one day's slackness, he knows he can drag you further.
Always maintain A Dairy/ Call Reports/ Log of:
- ✓ Date Phoned / Written / Contacted
- ✓ Reasons for Non – Payment
- ✓ Action Agreed
- ✓ Date to Chase up Again

At the end of it all, being professional pays in the long run…So your objective or motto should always be the following:

Finally in closing this chapter…Learn the Lessons!

When a Bad Debt occurs you need to ask some searching questions:

- Was it bad luck or bad judgment?
- Was the amount of debt bigger than it should have been?
- Would any reasonable steps have averted the bad debt?
- At what stage??
- Are there any lessons to be learnt for future?
- ✓

Handling turn downs/ rejections and keeping yourself motivated

After a series of calls where you sometimes may not achieve your objectives, it is quite natural to face call reluctance, sulk and withdraw. I have seen many collectors, who would gladly do anything but pick up the phone again and dial or hit the button for the next customer. This is normal. It happens when you take the rejection personally. Whatever happens, you cannot take rejection to heart- as even the rudest customers are actually not rejecting you personally. Fear of rejection is real and common. Recognize it and let it go.

Here are some ways to get yourself up and back again

- ✓ Take a few moments to meditate and clear your mind after a particularly difficult or frustrating call.
- ✓ Talk to a colleague about how you are feeling, and remember to be supportive to colleagues when they talk to you too.
- ✓ Understand collection call ratios: You should have a good idea of what the average closing ratio is in your industry so you can have realistic expectations. For example if you are aware that with every 1 in 5 calls usually results in a collection, it ensures that you set the right expectations by which to measure your success.
- ✓ Set your mind to remove the roadblocks that are holding you back from developing and

maintaining the attitude you need to achieve success.

✓ Instead of focusing on the negatives of rejection, it's important to think about how you can create positives from the situation. What did you learn from the whole situation? As well as helping to improve your mindset and make the working day even better, this positive attitude will be reflected in your success rate and could help you achieve more than you ever thought possible.

✓ Remember that competency and confidence are two key elements that allow sales and collection personnel to achieve success. If you have both, other obstacles can be overcome easily.

✓ Focus on solutions, not on problems- So concentrate on achieving success as opposed to worrying about failure.

✓ Keep reminding yourself of previous successes, and reward yourself even for reaching smaller goals.

✓ Before picking up the phone, envision yourself achieving success and closing more accounts. Focus on how you felt the last time you made a great and successful collection and recapture that feeling as you embark on making new calls.

✓ Visualize yourself succeeding: the customer appreciating you-your boss and colleagues applauding your efforts.

✓ Use positive self talk. It's garbage in: garbage out. If you feed your brain negative stuff, it affects your approach, our tone, your language and how you come across. So, practice positive self-talk (especially after rejection) and you'll experience less rejection in the first place.

- ✓ Encourage yourself to remember the last time you had a really good call just before making a fresh call. This will help to fuel enthusiasm when you make a call
- ✓ If you are a manager or supervisor of a collection team, develop a daily or weekly reward system or method of recognition for your top achievers. Give people something to work towards and motivate them with a friendly competition.
- ✓ Keep rewarding yourself for the successes you achieve in order to stay motivated and focused.
- ✓ Listen to talks of motivational speakers or read something that you find motivational.
- ✓ Try to surround yourself with positive people only who inspire and support you.
- ✓ Listen to upbeat music. This will help motivate you and keep you pepped up.
- ✓ Reinforce in your mind that by collecting money, you're not just helping yourself and your company; you're also helping your customers solve a problem.
- ✓ Everyone has their own goals that motivate them. It's important to determine what yours are early on and stay focused on them. Review your personal goals and objectives and focus on why you developed these goals. Make sure the goals you have are attainable. If, for example, you're saving money for a dream house or your marriage, picture that objective in your mind.

✓ Share success stories and be able to humorously look at the negative aspects of your job or situation in order to work through them and move on.

REMEMBER: Sales and collections are a people business and people buy people. Therefore, if you can maintain your positive attitude and apply some of these principles, not only will you be better placed to handle rejection, you'll experience less rejection in the first place and stay on top always!

Role-playing a Collection Call

The more you practice, the more you become an expert and a professional. So here are ways that you can practice role-playing at least twice a week. Keep doing this regularly and note what it does to your confidence and performance!

1. Work in teams of three or more to prepare for a role playing situation in which one will be the customer and the other the collector and the rest as observers.

2. A short script of the collection call should be prepared in which the collector is to have the following scenario as the call objective:

Your customer has purchased goods from your organization to the value of 55, 000 on the 13th of Jan 2023. The invoice was sent soon after. The payment was due after a 30 days credit period; ie; on the 14th of February 2023. It is now the 20th of February, and there are no signs of his payment.

3. Participants may use telephone equipment if available. If none is available, participants may role play their telephone conversation while sitting back to back so that they will not see each other, or they can be separated by a partition.

 4. Other members in the group may be observers and should critique the sales call by providing feedback on the positives, the areas of improvement- particularly in the steps of the collection call outlined, the voice (confidence, modulation etc), any distracting mannerisms displayed by the collector etc.

5. Each team should have the opportunity to role play their telephone conversation.

6. Recording the telephone conversations may be useful for assessing participant progress.

Additional situations can be developed for role playing- like:
1. *Calling the customer on the 13th February to remind about payment that is due the next day*
2. *After your call on the 20th February, with the customer assuring that payment would be sent in 2 days…It is now the 25th of February, and the money has still not come in.*

Taking this Forward!

Thank you for reading through this book. As you've now understood after reading this whole book, just because the economy is changing doesn't mean your sales and collections will automatically have to suffer. Sailing successfully through a downturn requires a great amount of diligence and skill than ever, and the benefits and rewards that come from it, can be much greater- as only the businesses that adapt to the situation with the right skills and strategies can not only survive and grow, but emerge much stronger than earlier, winning bigger share of the market by eating into the competitions share now!

It's crucial to always be ready for any type of crises, economic downturns, or other dangers to your company and work on recession-proofing your business as a proactive move, irrespective of whether a new downturn is imminent or you want to be ready "just in case."

Doing these things will provide excellent business results in good economic times and improve your ability to make it through the bad times. And yes, while business will certainly get harder, there's an upside to it. Opportunities that would otherwise be out of reach may become available during tough economic conditions and identifying and exploiting them may be the key to not only thriving in tough times but coming out stronger than ever before.

So as a leader, it's your responsibility to prepare for the worse by equipping your teams to weather any market condition-shifting from being reactive to proactive to ensure your business is resilient-whatever market upheaval lies ahead.

I am certain, that if you just follow the crucial steps outlined in this book with much discipline and dedication, when the market appears stuck, you'll keep moving forward. And when the market picks up pace, you'll have the momentum to cash in on opportunities that emerge.

So what's the next step?

As a Professional Collector, you would constantly need to remind yourself that 'Training is like Hygiene'! Just as how you would need to have a shower every day in order to stay fresh, so also you would need to keep yourself abreast and updated by constantly working on your skill sets and upgrading them from time to time. Just reading a book from cover to cover will not guarantee a change in the way you work. No idea or concept is worth anything, if it cannot be applied to real situations. So applying these principles by putting them to immediate practice is the KEY!

So how do you do that?

Well here are a few tips to help you do so…

- ✓ Set time to practice with Role-Plays!
- ✓ Maybe an hour a week- You could do it with your colleagues or someone you trust.
- ✓ Work on perfecting one step at a time! Don't aim to excel in all steps. One step at a time!
- ✓ Do periodic evaluation of your skills. See where you are today. Set a benchmark or standard to reach say in 3 months. Evaluate to see if you've moved in that direction.
- ✓ Keep this as a regular routine- Practice consistency!

- ✓ Read at least one book on 'Skill Development' a month and observe/ study Top Performers! There are many books…today even free pdf books that one could download.
- ✓ Remember my favorite saying: *"If you continue to do what you are always doing, you will continue to get what you are always getting"*
- ✓ In other words if we want something better than what we have today, we need to change our current style of working.

I do hope you've enjoyed and benefitted from this book. I thank you for your time and your desire to develop.

Should you have any Questions or any Suggestions that you'd want us to cover in a forthcoming book that can help you as well as others, feel free to write to: training@CollectionSkills.com

We wish you all Success…May you soar as an Eagle Collector!

Gerard Assey

About the Author
'GERARD ASSEY'

Gerard Assey is a Graduate in Economics, a PGD in Management (HRD) and holds a Doctorate in Leadership. Gerard holds several International Qualifications in Sales, Debt Collection, Training & Teaching, and is a 'Fellow' of the prestigious 'Institute of Sales & Marketing Management'-UK, a Certified NLP Practitioner, a 'Certified Trainer', an 'Accredited Management Teacher-Behavioral Sciences', a 'Certified Competency Facilitator', a 'Certified Management Consultant'- (the International credentials of a professional management consultant, awarded in accordance with global standards of the ICMCI); and a Certification from the University of Michigan in 'Successful Negotiation: Essential Strategies and Skills'

He is also a Member of the 'National Association of Sales Professionals' backed with several years experience in varied industries, both in India and Overseas. He also holds an 'Etiquette Consultant' Certification from the USA (by Sue Fox, Author of Best Seller: 'Business Etiquette for Dummies'. She has trained some of the top celebrities' world over). He was also a recipient of a scholarship for extensive training in Japan on 'Corporate Management for India'.

Gerard Assey is 'Founder & Chief Corporate Trainer' of the Group: **'Citius, Altius, Fortius Unlimited'**- an organization that **celebrates 22 years of Glorious Service** in 2023, focusing on 3 Core Competencies:

People. Performance. Profit; in functional areas of Sales & Marketing, HR & Organizational Development, covering Recruitment, Training & Consultancy!

Having managed organizations with large Sales Forces in India & Overseas, his specialization cover extensive areas of Sales Training (All levels - Presentation, Negotiation, Key/ Strategic Accounts Management & Managerial Skills for all sectors), Bid Proposal/ Capture Planning/ Management Trainings, Retail Sales, Customer Service & Customer Retention Programs, Training for Prevention & Collection of Debt, Self & Personal Development Programs (Time Management, Teamwork & Team Building, Business Etiquette & Personal Grooming, Leadership & Managerial Skills, People Management Skills, Train-the-Trainer etc), including preparation of Custom-designed Business Manuals for Internal (HR, Induction, and Sales etc) & External use (Instruction, User Manuals).

Gerard has successfully conducted over 5900 Trainings & Workshops (as of Feb '23) all across India, Middle East, Africa, Europe & S.E. Asia. Besides public programs conducted regularly, both in India & Overseas, he has some of the top names as clients whom he services from Single Owners to large Public & Government undertakings, covering all sectors, for their in-house needs.

His website: www.CollectionSkills.com is the only one in this part of the world to be featured in the 'Collections & Credit Risk Magazine-USA' under 'Who's Who in Training' and ranks TOP, along with other websites listed below on most search engines.

Gerard is author of 54 books already (Feb 2023),

A few of the business related books being:
1. Bite-sized Bits on Commonsense Management
2. Heart to Heart on Life's Principles'
3. How to become a Successful Manager
4. The Sales Professionals' Master Workbook of S.Y.S.T.E.M.S
5. The Professional Business Email Etiquette Handbook & Guide
6. The Professional Business Video-Conferencing Etiquette Handbook & Guide
7. Professional Presentation Skills
8. Exceptional Customer Service
9. Professional Tele-Marketing Skills
10. Professional Debt Collection Skills
11. The G.R.E.A.T. Sales & Service Workbook
12. Sales Training Advantage for Results (*The Ultimate Sales Training Manual
    to enable you stand out as a S.T.A.R.*)
13. CEO Daily Planner & Organizer
14. The Sales Professionals' Master Daily Planner
15. The Professional Debt Collector's Master Daily Planner
16. My Daily Planner & Organizer
17. MY EMERGENCY INFORMATION RECORD (Family Emergency & Peace of Mind Planner)
18. The Ultimate Therapist & Counselors Planner and Organizer
19. Building an Ethical Workplace
20. Managing Relationships at Work
21. Managing Business Meetings Effectively
22. Effective Delegation Skills
23. Goal Setting for Success
24. B2B Selling by Email
25. Professional Business Etiquette & Grooming
26. Dining Etiquette & Table Manners
27. Effective Networking Skills
28. Grooming, Etiquette & Manners for Teens, Young Adults & Future Leaders
29. InterPersonal Skills

30. Get Ready, Get Hired!
31. Selling in a Recession
32. Effective Receivables Management in an Economic Downturn!

Besides regularly contributing to business & trade journals, including international ones such as the 'Creative Training Techniques' and the 'Sales News' of the U.S.A, He is also a member of several prestigious bodies & trade associations, having participated in many Conferences & Workshops in India & Overseas.

Prior to his last assignment of leading & managing a large MNC as head, Gerard had a 3-year stint in the Middle East as a Consultant with a leading British Consultancy Firm.

As the past 'Official Country Representative' for the International Business Award- 'THE STEVIES'-(the business world's own Oscar) for about 4 years- he ensured a few Indian companies that qualify for the same every year!

Gerard can be contacted at:
Email: training@Sales-Training.in,training@CollectionSkills.com
Websites:

www.Sales-Training.in
www.EtiquetteWorks.in
www.CollectionSkills.com
www.RetailSalesTraining.in
www.SalesTrainingIndia.com
www.ManualPreparation.com
www.TrainingWithPuppets.com
www.FirstContactAcademy.com
www.SalesAndMarketingRecruiter.com

Our Debt Collection Training Programs

'**Collection Skills**'- as the name says, specializes in Training Programs for the Prevention & Collection of Debt and have been doing so for over 20 years now, serving customers from a diverse range of industries that include organizations that are Single Owners to large Public Multinationals & Government undertakings, covering all sectors- Manufacturing, Services, Financials, Telecom, FMCG's, and Projects & Contracting etc. with an impressive list of some of the top most names as its clients.

Part of a leading Training Group of Companies, the focus of this training is <u>not just</u> for the Collection of Debt (which is a reactive process), but <u>also for the Prevention part (the proactive!) as well</u>. This proactive part is like insurance for the health of an organization's future. If today an organization does have debt it is because it failed in the past on the preventive part!

'**Collection Skills**' conducts both Public & In-house sessions on the following topics, where the in-house sessions are tailor-made to suit the needs of any organization:

1) Master Program on: Prevention & Collection of Debt

2) Debt Collection Techniques (for any industry)

3) Debt Collection Techniques for Call Centers

4) Debt Collection Skills for Banks & Financial Institutions (for their Recovery Departments)

5) Debt Collection Supervisory Workshop

The '**Master Program on: Prevention & Collection of Debt**' focuses on the ultimate Retention of Customers, while educating participants to put in preventive measures for the future, thus covering the 4 KEY HOW's in Debt Collection:
HOW *bad debt occurs (An understanding on the impact of this in an organization)*
HOW *to prevent (Prevention is better than cure!)*
HOW *to collect your money…& finally*
HOW *to keep your customer!*

All our Programs are very innovative, participative, involving group discussions & exercises, group presentations, team games & role-plays to enhance involvement and active participation, thus leading to higher absorption that translates into action at the workplace.
Several organizations have remarked and attributed to the success of their turn-around in business, after having their staff & managers attend our training programs.

Don't just take our word; See what our

Customers have to say at:

http://www.CollectionSkills.com/Testimonials.html

More details can be seen on our website: www.CollectionSkills.com

Our **TRAININGS & BOOKS** that can help your team

- ✓ **Sales Effectiveness**: Selling Skills for any Sector: Service/ Logistics/ FMCG Realty/ Insurance & Finance/ Media/ SPA's, Health Clubs & Salons/ Key Account Management, Effective Negotiation Skills/ Bid & Proposal Management Skills/ Retail Sales Training: Any Sector (Auto, Jewelry, Clothing, Luxury etc)
- ✓ **Customer Service Skills**-Complaints Handling & Customer Retention
- ✓ **Debt Prevention & Collection Skills**
- ✓ **Etiquette & Grooming**
- ✓ **Leadership & Managerial Skills**
- ✓ **Self & Personal Development Skills**: Presentation Skills/ Effective Communication Skills/Business Proposal Writing Skills/ Problem Solving & Decision Making Skills/ Empowering Secretaries-The perfect PA! (For Secretaries & PA's)/ Effective Time Management/ Teamwork & Teambuilding/ P.R.I.D.E- **P**ersonal **R**esponsibility **I**n **D**elivering **E**xcellence

A Few of Our Business Books
By the Top Corporate Trainer & Author of 54 Books! (Feb '23)
And...DAILY PLANNERS for Every Corporate Need!
All Books available Online on all leading Stores in E-book & Paperback Formats
By the Top Corporate Trainer (Over 5900 workshops) & Author of 54 Published Books (Feb' 23)
Experts in Training for over 21 years:
Sales, Debt Prevention & Collection, Etiquette & Grooming , Leadership & Managerial Skills, Self & Personal Development Programs